SPECIAL OPS

JOURNAL OF THE ELITE FORCES
& SWAT UNITS
VOL.33

Ralph Zwilling

CONCORD
PUBLICATIONS COMPANY

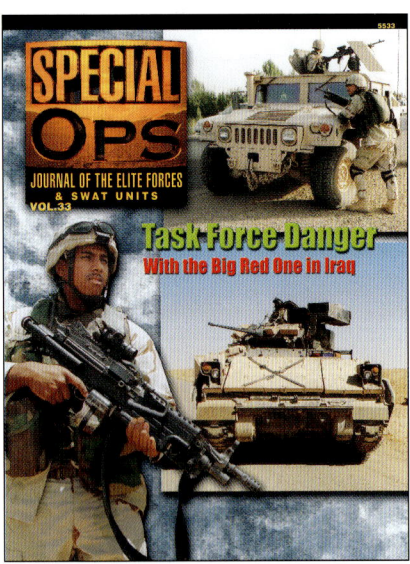

Editor:James R. Hill

Copyright © 2005

by CONCORD PUBLICATIONS CO.

603-609 Castle Peak Road

Kong Nam Industrial Building

10/F, B1, Tsuen Wan

New Territories, Hong Kong

www.concord-publications.com

We welcome authors who can help expand our range of books. If you would like to submit material, please feel free to contact us.

We are always on the look-out for new, unpublished photos for this series. If you have photos or slides or information you feel may be useful to future volumes, please send them to us for possible future publication. Full photo credits will be given upon publication.

ISBN 962-361-111-0

printed in Hong Kong

Introduction

On 20 March 2003, Coalition forces entered Iraq, forcing an end to the rule of the Ba'athist regime led by Saddam Hussein. The resulting conditions for the Iraqi population after the Iraq war were different than what had been speculated in the months leading up to the conflict. An acute humanitarian crisis did not materialize as anticipated. The predicted influx of refugees spilling over into neighboring Kuwait, Jordan and Turkey, and the projected degree of internal displacement due to the military campaign by Coalition forces, simply did not transpire. As a result, emergency preparedness efforts were ultimately applied not towards responding to emergency humanitarian needs due to military action and forced population movement, but rather to humanitarian needs resulting from increased civil insecurity, looting and years of neglect, isolation and oppression.

Despite U.S. President George W. Bush's official declaration aboard the aircraft carrier USS Abraham Lincoln on 1 May 2003 that the combat phase of the Iraq war was over and the rebuilding phase had began, there is still not a single day that international media organizations do not report about fighting between Iraqi insurgents and the U.S.-led Coalition troops, or about bomb attacks against Iraqi politicians, the Iraqi National Police (INP) or the Iraqi Civil Defense Corps (ICDC). Fifteen months after the United States led a coalition to oust Saddam Hussein from power, and two days before the 30 June deadline for control to be turned over to the interim Iraqi government, Iraq became a sovereign nation once more on Monday, 28 June 2004.

U.S. Ambassador L. Paul Bremer, who has overseen the Coalition Provisional Authority (CPA) since the fall of Saddam Hussein, signed the legal papers in the presence of Prime Minister Iyad Allawi and presented them to the chief justice of Iraq, Midhat al-Mahmoud. About a half dozen Iraqi and Coalition officials were also in attendance during this historical event in Baghdad. This transfer of authority was overshadowed by very violent and bloody skirmishes between insurgents, regime loyalists, Shiia militia, and terrorists on one side and the Coalition forces on the other. The new Iraqi Security Forces, consisting of INP, ICDC, as well as the newly formed Iraqi Army, Navy and Air Force are hardly able to control the security situation in the troubled state. One of the numerous car bomb attacks occurred at the main gate of Camp Summerall near Bayji in northern Iraq on 1 June,

killing 11 civilians, including seven members of the ICDC, and wounding 30. On the same day, U.S. troops were also involved in heavy fighting with militia of the Shi'ite leader, Moktada Al Sadr in the city of Kufa south of Baghdad.

The deadliest car bomb suicide attack prior to the transfer of authority took place on 17 June, when a car ripped into a throng of men waiting to sign up for the new Iraqi Army outside the Army's main recruiting station in the heart of Baghdad. Thirty-three people were killed and more than 127 were wounded. Also, after the official transfer of authority on 28 June 2004, the casualties continued to mount due to assassinations of members of the interim Iraqi government and bomb attacks against Coalition troops and the Iraqi people. On 17 July, a very powerful bomb exploded in the path of a convoy for Iraq's Minister of Justice, Malik Duhan Al Hasan, in Baghdad. The blast killed at least four Iraqis, two of whom were his bodyguards. The minister escaped unhurt.

Today, the situation in Iraq remains far from quiet and the new Iraqi Security and Defense Forces, as well as the Coalition troops are attacked daily. The rebuilding of the embargo- and war-shaken country has just started and will take many years. As of May 2004, over 114,000 U.S. personnel and over 23,000 Coalition personnel from over 30 nations were deployed in Iraq. More than 26,000 U.S. and Coalition personnel were deployed in Kuwait, providing logistical support to Operation "Iraqi Freedom 2." To stabilize and secure the situation in Iraq, U.S. troops normally based in Germany under command of the United States Army Europe (USAREUR) have been deployed to Iraq in order to support Operation "Iraqi Freedom 2." For nearly 15 months, elements of the 1st U.S. Armored Division "Old Ironsides" from Wiesbaden, Germany have been responsible for the security of Baghdad. Until 4 June 2004, Task Force 1st Armored Division secured some of Baghdad's roughest neighborhoods and brought stability to the city and its surrounding countryside. Since 16 March 2004, the 1st U.S. Infantry Division "Big Red One", which was originally headquartered in Würzburg, Germany, has controlled most of the "Sunni Triangle" north of Baghdad.

Join us in the following pages on a tour with the famous Big Red One in Iraq and experience a detailed look at the day-to-day missions of the Division's soldiers.

Organization of the Big Red One

The 1st U.S. Infantry Division is forward deployed as part of the United States Army Europe (USAREUR) and home based in Bavaria in the southern part of Germany. Its headquarters is at Leighton Barracks Würzburg, Germany, on the banks of the Main River in the middle of the Unterfranken wine-growing region of northern Bavaria. The Big Red One consists of more than 17,000 soldiers, who primarily serve in one of the Division's seven brigades or in one of its four separate battalions.

The 1st "Devil" Brigade is located at Fort Riley, Kansas, and its maneuver units consist of the 1st Battalion, 34th Armor; 2nd Battalion, 34th Armor; 1st Battalion, 16th Infantry; 1st Battalion, 5th Field Artillery; 1st Engineer Battalion; 101st Forward Support Battalion; C Battery, 4th Battalion, 3rd Air Defense Artillery; 331st Signal Company; and D Troop, 4th Cavalry.

The 2nd "Dagger" Brigade is headquartered at Conn Barracks Schweinfurt, Germany. Its maneuver units are the 1st Battalion, 18th Infantry; 1st Battalion, 26th Infantry; 1st Battalion, 77th Armor; and E Troop, 4th Cavalry.

The 3rd "Duke" Brigade is headquartered at Rose Barracks in Vilseck northeast of Bavaria. Its maneuver units are the 1st Battalion, 63rd Armor; 2nd Battalion, 63rd Armor; 2nd Battalion, 2nd Infantry; and F Troop, 4th Cavalry.

The 4th "Dragon" Brigade, or Aviation Brigade, headquartered at the Katterbach Kaserne in Ansbach, Germany, southwest of Nuremberg, consists of the 1st and 2nd Battalions, 1st Aviation.

The Division Artillery "Drumfire" is headquartered at Warner Barracks Bamberg, Germany, and consists of the 1st Battalion, 6th Field Artillery and the 1st Battalion, 33rd Field Artillery (MLRS/TA), both headquartered in Bamberg, and the 1st Battalion, 7th Field Artillery headquartered in Schweinfurt.

The Division Engineer Brigade "Devastator" and the 82nd Engineer Battalion are headquartered at Warner Barracks, while the 9th Engineer Battalion is headquartered at Ledward Barracks in Schweinfurt. The Division Support Command "Durable," which is headquartered in Kitzingen, is made up of the 201st Forward Support Battalion at Rose Barracks, the 299th Forward Support Battalion at Ledward Barracks, the 601st Aviation Support Battalion at Katterbach Kaserne, and the 701st Main Support Battalion at Harvey Barracks in Kitzingen.

The 4th Battalion, 3rd Air Defense Artillery and the 121st Signal Battalion are headquartered at Larson Barracks in Kitzingen, while the 101st Military Intelligence Battalion and the 1st Military Police Company are headquartered at nearby Würzburg's Leighton Barracks. The 1st Squadron, 4th Cavalry, the Big Red One's organic reconnaissance and security force, is based at Conn Barracks in Schweinfurt. The 12th Chemical Company has its home station in Kitzingen, while the 1st ID Band is stationed in Bamberg.

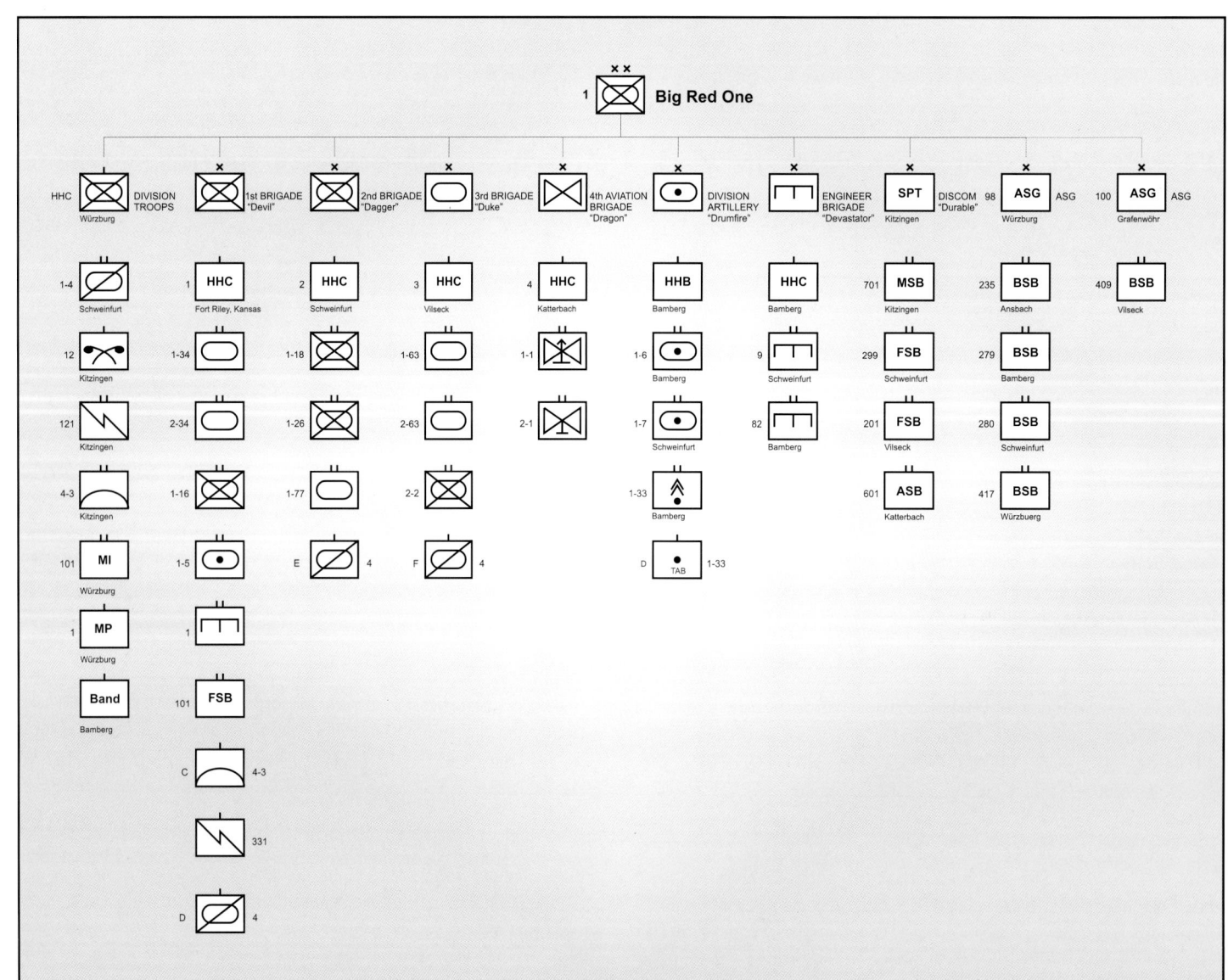

History of the Big Red One

World War I (1914 – 1918)

The 1st U.S. Infantry Division is the oldest continuously serving division in the United States Army. The Big Red One has had many roles that helped shape the country's history. The First Division was enacted into the U.S. Army as Headquarters, First Expeditionary Division, on 24 May 1917. It was organized in May 1917 from Army units then in service on the Mexican border and at various Army posts throughout the United States. It was officially organized on 8 June 1917 under the command of Brig. Gen. William L. Sibert. The first units sailed from New York and Hoboken, New Jersey, on 14 June 1917. Throughout the remainder of the years, the rest of the Division followed, landing in St. Nazaire, France and Liverpool, England. After a brief stay in rest camps, the troops in England proceeded to France, landing at Le Havre. The last units arrived in St. Nazaire on 22 December.

Upon arrival in France, the Division – minus the Artillery – was assembled in the 1st (Gondrecourt) Training Area and the Artillery at Le Valdahon. On the 4th of July, the 2nd Battalion, 16th Infantry, paraded through the streets of Paris to bolster the sagging French spirits. At Lafayette's tomb, one of General Pershing's staff uttered the famous words, "Lafayette, we are here!" Two days later, on 6 July, the First Expeditionary Division was re-designated as the First Infantry Division.

On the morning of 23 October, the first American shell of the war was sent screaming toward German lines by a First Division artillery unit. Two days later, the 2nd Battalion, 16th Infantry, suffered the first American casualties of the war. The last major World War I battle was fought in the Meuse-Argonne Forest. The Division advanced seven kilometers and defeated, in whole or part, eight German divisions. The war came to a close when the Armistice was signed on 11 November 1918. The Division was at Sedan, the farthest American penetration of the war. The Division was the first to cross the Rhine into occupied Germany. By the end of the war, the Division had suffered 22,320 casualties and boasted five Medals of Honor winners.

World War II (1941 – 1945)

The 1st Infantry Division entered World War II at Oran, North Africa, as part of the Operation "Torch" invasion, the first American campaign against Germany. On 8 November 1942, following training in the United Kingdom, men of the First Division landed on the coast of Algeria near Oran. The initial lessons of combat were harsh, and many men were casualties in the following campaign in Tunisia. On 9 May 1943, the commander of the German *Afrika Korps* surrendered his force of 40,000. The Division then moved on to take Sicily in Operation "Husky." The 1st Infantry Division stormed ashore at Gala on 10 July 1943 and quickly overpowered the Italian tanks from the Herman Göring *Panzer* Division.

On D-Day, 6 June 1944, the Big Red One stormed ashore at Omaha Beach. Soon after H-Hour, the Division's 16th Regiment was fighting for its life on a strip of beach near Coleville-sur-Mer that had been marked "Easy Red" on the battle maps. The beach was so congested with the dead and dying that there was no room to land reinforcements. Colonel George Taylor, commander of the 16th Infantry Regiment, told his men, "Two kinds of people are staying on this beach! The dead and those who are going to die! Now, let's get the hell out of here!" Slowly, the move inland got under way. A German blockhouse above the beach became a command post and was named "Danger Forward."

The Division moved through the Normandy hedgerows, liberated Liege, Belgium, and pushed on to the German border, crossing through the Siegfried Line. The 1st Infantry Division attacked the first major German city, Aachen, and after days of bitter fighting, the German commander surrendered the city on 21 October 1944.

The Division continued its push into Germany, crossing the Rhine River. On 16 December, twenty-four enemy divisions, ten of which were armored, launched a massive counterattack in the Ardennes sector, resulting in what became known as the Battle of the Bulge. On 15 January 1945, the 1st Infantry Division attacked and penetrated the Siegfried Line for the second time and occupied the Remagen bridgehead. The enemy did not expect an attack to be launched in the snow and cold on 25 February when the Big Red One crossed the Roer River and began the Rheinland offensive. On 16 March 1945, the Division crossed the Weser River in Czechoslovakia.

The war ended on 8 May 1945. At the end of World War II, the Division had suffered 21,023 casualties, and 43,743 men had served in its ranks. Its soldiers had won a total of 20,752 medals and awards, including 16 Congressional Medals of Honor. Over 100,000 prisoners had been taken. Following the war, the First Division remained in Germany as occupation troops until 1955, when the Division moved to Fort Riley, Kansas.

Vietnam War (1965 – 1970)

In 1965, the First Infantry Division was again selected to be the first division to be deployed, this time to Vietnam. The first unit to go was the 2nd Brigade. Advance parties landed at Qui Nhon on 23 June 1965. For nearly five years, First Infantry Division soldiers battled against an aggressive enemy who made expert use of the dense jungles and inaccessible countryside. The use of helicopters was one of the best means of countering the jungle and the lack of roads. The experience gained in re-supply operations, medical evacuation and the tactics of airmobile assault was applied in developing basic doctrine in these areas.

The First Infantry Division returned to Fort Riley in April 1970. More than 2,000 soldiers of the Big Red One died in action. Eleven Medal of Honor winners were added to the roles. Home again, the Big Red One became a dual-base division with its 3rd Brigade in West Germany. The Division was credited with another first when it embarked on the beginning of long series of REFORGER (Return of Force to Germany) exercises. These exercises demonstrated the U.S. determination and capability to defend, with the NATO allies, Western Europe.

Persian Gulf War (1990 – 1991)

On 2 August 1990, Iraq invaded Kuwait. This act precipitated U.S. military involvement in the Persian Gulf. The 1st Infantry Division was put on alert for deployment on 8 November 1990. The Division deployed over 12,000 soldiers and 7,000 pieces of equipment to Saudi Arabia over the next two months. On the morning of 24 February 1991, the Big Red One, under the command of Maj. Gen. Thomas G. Rhame, spearheaded the armored attack into Iraq, leading the way for the VII Corps. The Division smashed into the Iraqi 26th Infantry Division by breaking through the enemy lines and taking more than 2,500 prisoners. At 0800 on 28 February 1991, the war came to an end when a cease-fire was called.

The Big Red One had fought through 260 kilometers (161.5 miles) of enemy-held territory in 100 hours, destroying 550 enemy tanks, 480 armored personnel carriers and taking 11,400 prisoners. Eighteen of the Division's soldiers paid the ultimate sacrifice. On 10 May 1990, the Division unfurled its colors at Fort Riley, signifying its return home.

Task Force Eagle – Bosnia

On 10 April 1996, the colors of the 1st Infantry Division moved to the German city of Würzburg. Shortly after their arrival, the soldiers of the Big Red One assumed peace-enforcement responsibilities in Bosnia-Herzegovina in support of Operation "Joint Endeavor/Guardian." Units of the 1st Infantry Division played a key role in Bosnia. The 1st Squadron, 4th Cavalry Regiment was attached to 2nd Brigade, 1st U.S. Armored Division "Old Ironsides" during Operation "Joint Endeavor" from October 1995 to October 1996. The Squadron crossed the Sava River on 3 January 1996 and led the 2nd Brigade Combat Team into Bosnia. The 1st ID assumed authority for command and control of Task Force Eagle in a transfer-of-authority ceremony at Eagle Base on 10 November 1996. The Division's mission was to provide a covering force for the 1st U.S.

Armored Division units returning to Germany and to continue to implement the military aspects of the General Framework Agreement for Peace.

The 1st ID continued to support the Dayton Peace Accord through the transition from the Implementation Force (IFOR) to the Stabilization Force (SFOR) in December of 1996, along with National Guard and Reserve soldiers, members of the Navy, Air Force and Marines, and the soldiers from 12 nations in the area known as Multinational Division North (MND [N]).

Task Force Falcon – Kosovo

Task Force Falcon was formed on 5 February 1999 when the 1st Infantry Division was notified of a possible deployment to conduct peace-support operations in Kosovo. The Division deployed to the Balkans twice in 1999, first as part of Task Force Sabre in Macedonia, then in Kosovo with NATO's Task Force Falcon. Advance elements of TF Falcon entered Kosovo on 10 June 1999 as part of Operation "Joint Guardian," a NATO-led peacekeeping force. This contingent patrolled the streets and countryside of Kosovo until June 2000, when it turned the mission over to the 1st U.S. Armored Division.

Operation Iraqi Freedom

By mid-October 2002, the 1st Infantry Division's parent command – the Heidelberg, Germany-based V Corps headquarters – was on its way to Kuwait, along with a battalion of Apache helicopters and a corps-level Marine command post. But the 1st Infantry Division faced six months of retraining before the first units would be available for combat deployment against Iraq. The Division's 2nd "Dagger" Brigade task force was wrapping up a six-month tour of duty in Kosovo, and the Division's 3rd "Duke" Brigade was preparing to relieve these soldiers in November 2002 for their own half-year tour. A key part of the brigade, the Division's 1st

Squadron, 4th Cavalry Regiment, was given last-minute orders to remain in Germany. For 1st Infantry Division soldiers to take part in an Iraqi attack, the incoming 3rd Brigade would have to get a last minute re-tasking for combat duty, or the outgoing 2nd Brigade would have to be put through a crash retraining program.

In November 2002, the 2nd Battalion, 63rd Armor Regiment joined NATO's Task Force Falcon in support of Operation "Joint Guardian" for a peacekeeping mission in Kosovo. The 2-63 Armor enforced peace agreements in the Multinational Brigade East sector. It also helped to create a more secure environment and assisted in transition of civilian control.

In January 2003, the Division primed itself for Operation "Iraqi Freedom." Big Red One soldiers formed Headquarters, Armed Forces-Turkey (AFOR-T) and prepared the way for the 4th U.S. Infantry Division to enter Iraq through Turkey. When the Turkish government denied access through their border, AFFOR-T collapsed the line of communication it had built and the 4th ID deployed to Iraq via Kuwait. The Division took a more direct role in Operation "Iraqi Freedom" in March 2003, when the 1st Battalion, 63rd Armor Regiment from Vilseck, Germany, deployed to Northern Iraq to support the Southern European Task Force (SETAF). Operating in the Sunni Triangle, Task Force 1-63 conducted combat operations while simultaneously helping bring stability to the region. As TF 1-63 returned home to Germany in February 2004, the rest of the 1st U.S. Infantry Division and Task Force Danger deployed to Northern Iraq in support of Operation "Iraqi Freedom 2." For this operation, the 1st Infantry Division's Task Force Danger consists of Germany-based 1st ID units, along with the 30th Brigade Combat Team "Old Hickory" (based in North Carolina) and the 25th Infantry Division's 2nd Brigade Combat Team, as well as several other elements of the Army National Guard.

From Germany to Iraq

For the 1st U.S. Infantry Division Operation "Iraqi Freedom 2" began back in the summer of 2003 when the unit received its orders to prepare for a deployment to Iraq. In July 2003, Following a long period of preparation of vehicle maintenance, mission rehearsal exercises, and extensive training at the Grafenwöhr Training Area (GTA), the Combat Maneuver Training Center (CMTC) and at home stations throughout Bavaria, Germany, which began in July 2003, the first elements of the 1st U.S. Infantry Division were deployed to Camp Udairi in Kuwait in January 2004. On 30 January 2004, the V Corps' 1st U.S. Infantry Division hosted a ceremony at Leighton Barracks in Würzburg to mark its upcoming deployment to Iraq in support of Operation "Iraqi Freedom 2." Along with many German politicians and regional high officials, the Bavarian Minister President Dr. Edmund Stoiber joined the ceremony. At the completion of the ceremony, Major General John R.S. Batiste dedicated a "Victory Tree" as a symbol of the division's commitment to return to Germany in one year. This tree will remain lit until every Big Red One soldier returns from Operation "Iraqi Freedom 2."

When units like the Big Red One deploy from their home stations, everything must be in order so there are no maintenance faults or documentation problems. This review process makes it easier to fix a problem at the home station so that you do not find out you have a problem at a port or at the final destination. Thousands of vehicles were processed through the Installation Staging Areas (ISA), then sent to bases throughout Bavaria, and each one of them went through an elaborate inspection process to ensure that it was ready to deploy to Iraq. After the ISA checks, the equipment was transported by numerous convoys, rail cars and barges from the different home stations to overseas harbors in Belgium, it was finally prepared and shipped to Southwest Asia. In every case, the exact weight and measurements of each vehicle was very important. But size and weight weren't the only things checked before the vehicles were cleared through ISA. Things such as the vehicle's safety and environmental readiness were also checked. Each vehicle was put through a five-station

process, and at each station the vehicle had to go through a laundry list of items that had to be checked and passed before it would be able to move on to the next station.

Supported by the 21st Theater Support Command (TSC), approximately 17,000 soldiers deployed by air on military and chartered commercial aircraft directly from Germany to Kuwait. In Camp Udairi, Kuwait, the Big Red One soldiers concentrated on individual training, refining standard operating procedures and conducting many soldier-led classes while waiting for the arrival of their vehicles from the port in Kuwait City. Most of these classes revolved around IED awareness, first aid, rules of engagement, lessons that were learned, and Arabic culture and language. But the soldiers also trained Convoy Live Fire Exercises as the Tactical Approach March from Kuwait into Iraq was expected to be very dangerous and difficult.

Probably the most rewarding training for the soldiers was the three days spent conducting Close Quarters Marksmanship (CQM). For many of the soldiers, this was their first time moving through a building and firing live ammunition in close proximity to targets while firing right next to their fellow team-mates. These live-fire building-clearing exercises were done both day and night to give soldiers the most realistic training available. After this training, a display of confidence (which was not present before) began to bolster these soldiers as most of their first-round jitters and worries about using their weapons alongside their battle buddies vanished. Another confidence builder was the issue of the Small Arms Protective Insert (SAPI) plates for the recently introduced Interceptor Body Armor (IBA). The soldiers did not mind the initial irritation or carrying the additional weight of 4kg (9 lbs.) because the plates might save their life in the future.

The equipment of the 1st U.S. Infantry Division arrived with several ships in late February and was unloaded immediately at the Seaport of

The first elements from the 1st Battalion, 26th Infantry Regiment "Blue Spaders" conducted rail load operations with their M2A2 ODS Bradley infantry fighting vehicles on 23 January 2004 at Conn Barracks in Schweinfurt, Germany in preparation for the 1st ID's deployment to Iraq in support of Operation "Iraqi Freedom 2." The new side stowage racks for the M2A2 ODS Bradleys, issued in November 2003, were removed and stowed separately during the loading operations because the width of the vehicles with attached racks would have been too great for the German railways. Since the Bradley IFVs received the Explosive Reactive Armor in the camps in Kuwait, the side stowage racks were not installed for the mission in Iraq and are now used by M113A3 APCs.

A 1st U.S. Infantry Division soldier conducts close quarters marksmanship training with his 5.56mm M16A2 rifle on 22 February 2004 at Udairi Range. Soldiers participated in three days of training, which culminated in a convoy live fire operation on 23 February 2004. After this training, a display of confidence, which was not present before, began to take over these soldiers, and most of the first round jitters and worries about using their weapons next to their battle buddies were gone. (1st ID PAO)

In Camp Udairi, Kuwait, soldiers from the 1st Squadron, 4th U.S. Cavalry "Quarterhorse" concentrated on individual training, refining standard operating procedures and conducting many soldier-led classes while waiting for the arrival of their vehicles from the port in Kuwait City. (1st ID PAO)

A scout from the 1st U.S. Infantry Division's Anvil Troop, 1st Squadron, 4th Cavalry Regiment boresights his 25mm gun prior to zeroing his Bradley fighting vehicle at Udairi Range. Shortly after the arrival in Kuwait and prior to the deployment to Iraq, all M2A2 ODS and M3A2 ODS received the new Explosive Reactive Armor to protect the vehicles against the rising threat of RPGs (rocket-propelled grenades) and IEDs (improvised explosive devices). (1st ID PAO)

Debarkation (SPOD) in Kuwait. Over 7,000 pieces of equipment were moved into the theater of operations, including Abrams tanks, Bradley infantry fighting vehicles, howitzers, up-armored HMMWVs, and both armed reconnaissance and attack helicopters. The equipment was unloaded from ships, then quickly organized by unit and configured with crews. All vehicles and aircraft went through a screening process to ensure that they were capable of firing their primary weapons systems.

The only thing left to do after loading all the vehicles and containers was to wait for the order to move north into Iraq to replace the 4th U.S. Infantry Division "Ivy Division". The exact date was kept a secret for security purposes and was only disseminated a few hours prior to departure. The order came on 27 February, and C Troop, 1st Squadron, 4th U.S. Cavalry "Quarterhorse" was first in the order to march into Iraq. All the combat vehicles of the troop, which is part of the Division's reconnaissance and security force, were loaded on Heavy Equipment Transport Systems (HETS) belonging to a Kansas Army National Guard transportation unit for the long ride from Camp Udairi, Kuwait to Logistic Supply Area (LSA) Anaconda, which was located 68km (42 miles) northwest of Baghdad. The rest of the 1st U.S. Infantry Division followed in numerous convoys during the following days. Before the deployment of the Division elements, Task Force Danger leadership conducted multiple reconnaissance missions in the area of operations in order to gain situational awareness, conduct deliberate rehearsals, and establish relationships that are conducive to sharing information and lessons learned.

During Operation "Iraqi Freedom 2," the mission of the 1st ID and Task Force Danger, in full partnership with Iraqi civil and military authorities, is to continue to ensure a secure, stable and self-reliant Iraq. Simultaneously, the Task Force conducts full-spectrum operations throughout the area of operations in order to neutralize anti-Iraqi forces and set the conditions for successful national elections. This M1A1 AIM Abrams main battle tank belonging to Task Force 1-77 was seen south of Balad in May 2004 during a combat patrol. Before the deployment to Iraq, the Division planned to employ most of the soldiers in an infantry role. Therefore, the units were mostly equipped with up-armored M1114 HMMWVs when they left Germany, and only a few M1A1 AIM tanks and M2A2/M3A2 ODS Bradley infantry fighting vehicles were shipped to Southwest Asia.

More than a decade after leading the charge into Iraq during Operation "Desert Storm," the 1st U.S. Infantry Division returned to the region in February 2004 to begin another chapter in its rich heritage. The Big Red One officially assumed command of Tikrit and the surrounding area from the 4th U.S. Infantry Division during a transfer-of-authority ceremony on 16 March 2004. Lt. Gen. Ricardo S. Sanchez, U.S. commander of the allied forces in Iraq and commander of V Corps, as well as other American military and Iraqi luminaries attended the event. This photo shows Major General John R.S. Batiste and Command Sergeant Major Cory McCarty uncasing the 1st U.S. Infantry Division colors during the transfer-of-authority ceremony at Forward Operating Base Danger in Tikrit, Iraq. (SPC Sherree Capser, 196th MPAD)

During Operation "Iraqi Freedom 2," the headquarters of the 1st U.S. Infantry Division is located in Tikrit. Situated 150km (93 miles) northwest of Baghdad and covering four square kilometers, this is the largest and most elaborate of the presidential sites. In addition to 18 palaces and VIP residences, the site also includes farms and rural retreats for VIPs located farther to the west. Construction at the Tikrit residential site had been ongoing since 1991. From here the Division, under command of Major General John R.S. Batiste and Command Sergeant Major Cory McCarty, leads the division troops and the four attached combat brigades. The Big Red One officially assumed command of Tikrit and the surrounding area from the 4th U.S. Infantry Division "Ivy Division" during a transfer-of-authority ceremony on 16 March 2004. Lt. Gen. Ricardo S. Sanchez, U.S. commander of allied forces in Iraq and the V Corps commander, and other high-ranking American officers and Iraqi dignitaries attended the event. Media organizations from around the world were also at the ceremony, which was held on the stairs of the main palace at Forward Operating Base Danger.

The Area of Responsibility (AOR) consists of the four provinces (Salah Ad Din, Kirkuk, Diyala and As Sulaymaniyah) located north of Baghdad, home of more than 3,496,500 inhabitants. The majority of the population in the AOR are Sunni Muslims and Kurds, but there are also strong proportions of Shi'ite Muslim and Turkomen living in the AOR. The major cities in the AOR of the Big Red One are Tikrit, Bayji, Samarra, Balad, Jalula, Kirkuk, Taji and Baqubah. Tikrit, located on the Tigris River northwest of Baghdad, is Saddam Hussein's birthplace, where his clan and tribe are still predominant. But it is also the birthplace of Salah Al Din al Ayubi, a Kurdish warrior and, later, the Sultan of Egypt and champion of Islam, who became a legend in the East and West for his role in driving the Crusaders from Jerusalem. Many of Saddam's ruling elite hailed from Tikrit because he wanted to surround himself with people he could trust. Since the early 1970s, Saddam Hussein had fortified his position by recruiting young men from his hometown, and his innermost circle was only recruited from the Al Bu Nasir tribe to which Saddam belonged.

Both Bayji and Tikrit are located along Highway 1 – named Main Supply Route "Tampa" – which is used to re-supply all of the U.S. Forces in northern Iraq, and which is attacked daily with numerous IEDs. The city of Bayji, which is located 250km (155 miles) northwest of Baghdad and has a population of 25,000 inhabitants, is a critical communication link between Baghdad and northern Iraq. Also, it has the largest thermal power plant in the country, which is a major contributor to Baghdad's electricity supply. The Al-Bayji refinery, with its production capacity of 290,000-300,000 barrels per day, is one of three major refineries in Iraq and is connected by pipeline to the oilfields of Kirkuk.

A major hot spot in the AOR of the 1st U.S. Infantry Division is Samarra, a 250,000-inhabitants-strong city that has an outstanding religious importance for the Shi'ites due to two important shrines situated in the city. Despite this fact, the local population is mainly composed of Sunni that support the old regime. In Samarra, attacks on U.S. troops are a daily event, and these attacks often culminate in daylong gunfights between local fighters and soldiers of the Big Red One. In Baqubah, a town in central eastern Iraq located on the Diyala River, U.S. Forces are attacked daily by Iraqi insurgents and regime loyalists with mortars, small arms and IEDs. On a road and rail line between Baghdad and Iran, it is the regional trade center for agricultural products and livestock.

Conducting combat patrols on Highway 1 and performing body checks on suspicious people are just two of the various missions of the Task Force Danger soldiers while deployed to Iraqi during Operation "Iraqi Freedom 2." Here, while one soldier searches the driver and the passenger of a commercial Iraqi truck, his buddy provides security with a 5.56mm M16A4 rifle.

During Operation "Iraqi Freedom 2," the headquarters of the 1st U.S. Infantry Division is located in Tikrit. Located 150km (93 miles) northwest of Baghdad, this is the largest and most elaborate of the presidential sites. From here the Division, under command of Major General John R.S. Batiste and Command Sergeant Major Cory McCarty, leads the Division troops and the four attached combat brigades.

Major General John R.S. Batiste, Lieutenant Colonel David S. Hubner Sr. and Command Sergeant Major John W. Fortune are shown during a Purple Heart ceremony at LSA Anaconda on 29 May 2004.

Major General John R. S. Batiste, who took command of the 1st ID in July 2002, was commissioned as an infantry officer upon graduation in 1974 from the United States Military Academy. He graduated from U.S. Army Airborne and Ranger schools and is authorized to wear the Expert Infantryman Badge and the Combat Infantryman Badge. His decorations include the Defense Superior Service Medal with one Oak Leaf Cluster, Legion of Merit with one Oak Leaf Cluster, Bronze Star, Meritorious Service Medal with four Oak Leaf Clusters, Army Commendation Medal, and the Army Achievement Medal.

But there are also quiet spots in the AOR of the 1st U.S. Infantry Division; one of these is Kirkuk. Controlled by Kurdish politicians and Kurdish militia (which are monitored by a small contingent of U.S. troops), the city is located close to one of the largest oil fields in Iraq. During Operation "Iraqi Freedom 2," the mission of the 1st U.S. Infantry Division and Task Force Danger – in full partnership with Iraqi civil and military authorities – is to continue to ensure a secure, stable and self-reliant Iraq. Simultaneously, the Task Force conducts full-spectrum operations throughout the area of operations in order to neutralize anti-Iraqi forces and set the conditions for successful national elections. The soldiers of the Big Red One are prepared to neutralize or capture the enemy while simultaneously setting the conditions for Iraqi military and civil self-reliance. In concert with Iraqi Security Forces, the Division will establish a safe and secure environment to set conditions for a transfer of operations to designated follow-on military or civilian authorities.

The Big Red One is also responsible for training the new Iraqi Security Forces and support reconstruction of the civilian infrastructure. The Division was reorganized to accomplish this complex mission in Iraq, and it received support from elements of the Army National Guard that are normally based in the United States. At the time of writing, the 1st U.S. Infantry Division and Task Force Danger consisted of the following Active Army and Army National Guard units.

This photo shows Lieutenant Colonel David S. Hubner Sr., Commander of the 1st Battalion, 77th Armor Regiment "Steel Tigers" and Task Force 1-77, together with an honor guard during the Memorial Day ceremony on 31 May 2004 in Forward Operating Base Paliwoda. Memorial Day, originally called Decoration Day, is a day of remembrance for those who have died in service of the United States of America. During the ceremony, LTC Hubner delivered a very personal and emotional speech. His battalion had already lost several soldiers during Operation "Iraqi Freedom 2."

Division Troops
- Headquarters and Headquarters Company, 1st U.S. Infantry Division
- 1st Squadron, 4th Cavalry Regiment (M1A1 AIM Abrams MBT, M3A2 ODS Bradley CFV, OH-58D (I) Kiowa Warrior)
- 4th Battalion, 3rd Air Defense Artillery Regiment (M2A2 ODS Bradley SFV, Stinger MANPAD, Avenger)
- 101st Military Intelligence Battalion
- 121st Signal Battalion
- 106th Finance Battalion
- 38th Personnel Support Battalion
- 415th Civil Affairs Battalion
- 2 ASOS
- 1st Military Police Company (HMMWV)
- 12th Chemical Company (M 93A1 Fox NBCRS, M1053A3)

2nd "Dagger" Brigade Combat Team
- 1st Battalion, 18th Infantry Regiment (M2A2 ODS Bradley IFV)
- 1st Battalion, 26th Infantry Regiment (M2A2 ODS Bradley IFV))
- 1st Battalion, 77th Armor Regiment (M1A1 AIM Abrams MBT)
- 2nd Battalion, 108th Infantry Regiment, New York Army National Guard
- 1st Battalion, 7th Field Artillery Regiment (M109A6 sPH)
- 9th Engineer Battalion (M9 ACE, SEE, M60 AVLB, MICLIC)
- 299th Forward Support Battalion

3rd "Duke" Brigade Combat Team
- 2nd Battalion, 2nd Infantry Regiment (M2A2 ODS Bradley IFV)
- 2nd Battalion, 63rd Armor Regiment (M1A1 AIM Abrams MBT)

Exactly 60 years after the soldiers of the Big Red One landed at Omaha Beach in Normandy on 6 June 1944 during WWII, Brigadier General John W. Morgan III hands the 1st ID Combat Patch, officially known as the Shoulder Sleeve Insignia indicating Former Wartime Service, to Command Sergeant Major Robert S. Winzenried, who belongs to the 1st ID Engineer Brigade, at Forward Operating Base Danger in Tikrit, Iraq. The awarding of combat patches to soldiers is a tradition that dates back to World War II.

- 1st Battalion, 6th Field Artillery Regiment (M109A6 SPH)
- 82nd Engineer Battalion (M9 ACE, SEE, M60 AVLB, MICLIC)
- 201st Forward Support Battalion

30th "Old Hickory" Brigade Combat Team
(North Carolina Army National Guard)
- 1st Battalion, 120th Infantry Regiment (M2A2 ODS Bradley IFV)
- 1st Battalion, 150th Armor Regiment (M1A1 AIM Abrams MBT)
- 1st Battalion, 252nd Armor Regiment (M1A1 AIM Abrams MBT)
- 1st Battalion, 113th Field Artillery Regiment (M109A6 SPH)
- 105th Engineer Battalion (M9 ACE, SEE, M60 AVLB, MICLIC)
- 230th Forward Support Battalion

2nd Brigade, 25th Infantry Division "Warriors"
- 1st Battalion, 14th Infantry Regiment
- 1st Battalion, 21st Infantry Regiment
- 1st Battalion, 27th Infantry Regiment
- 2nd Battalion, 11th Field Artillery
- 225th Forward Support Battalion

4th "Dragon" Brigade
- 1st Battalion, 1st Aviation (AH-64A Apache)
- 2nd Battalion, 2nd Aviation (UH-60L Black Hawk)
- 601st Aviation Support Battalion

Division Artillery "Drumfire"
- 1st Battalion, 33rd Field Artillery Regiment (M270 MLRS; AN/TPQ-36, AN/TPQ-37)

Division Engineers "Devastator"
- Headquarters and Headquarters Detachment ENGR BDE

Division Support "Durable"
- 701st Main Support Battalion

264th Corps Engineer Group (Wisconsin Army National Guard)
- 216th Engineer Battalion
- 141st Engineer Battalion

167th Corps Support Group (U.S. Army Reserve)
- 44th Corps Support Battalion
- 232nd Corps Support Battalion
- 835th Corps Support Battalion

To accomplish its complex mission in Iraq, the Division was reorganized, and it received support from elements of the Army National Guard, who are normally based in the United States. At the time of writing, the 1st ID and Task Force Danger consisted of Active Army and Army National Guard units. Staff Sergeant Derocher, who is armed with a 5.56mm M4A1 carbine with an AN/PEQ-2A aiming light, belongs to Bravo Company of the 2nd Battalion, 108th Infantry Regiment "Hunters" based at LSA Anaconda.

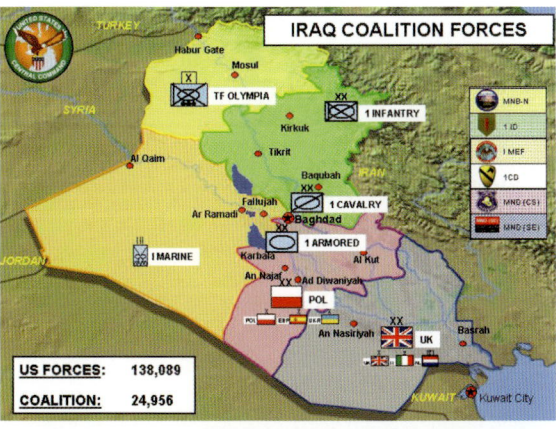

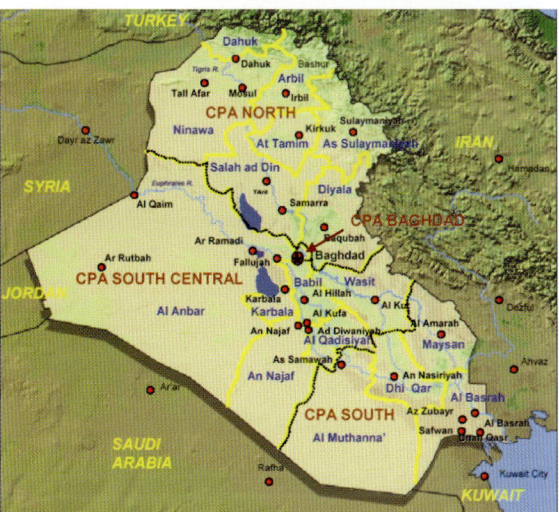

Today, U.S. Army National Guard units are trained and equipped just like active U.S. Army units, but they have two missions: they can be activated by their state for state emergencies or federalized and deployed by the national government. Active and Reserve troops have strong similarities, including a professional attitude, unit cohesion and a strong sense of mission.

The 2nd "Dagger" Brigade Combat Team, with its headquarters in FOB Dagger near Tikrit, is responsible for the Salah Ad Din province west of the Tigris River. The eastern sector of the province is controlled by the 1st Squadron, 4th Cavalry Regiment, which is based at FOB McKenzie east of Samarra. The 3rd "Duke" Brigade Combat Team, which has its area of operation in the western sector of the Diyala province, is located in FOB Warhorse near Baqubah. The eastern part of the province is controlled by the 30th "Old Hickory" Brigade Combat Team from FOB Caldwell. The 2nd Brigade, 25th Infantry Division "Warrior", with its headquarters in FOB Warrior in Kirkuk, is responsible for the provinces of Kirkuk and As Sulaymaniyah, which boast a combined population of more than 1,500,000 people.

The 1st "Devil" Brigade, which is usually based at Fort Riley, Kansas, deployed to Iraq in September 2003 and is currently based in Ramadi, where the brigade supports the 1st Marine Expeditionary Force. To successfully accomplish the mission in Iraq, the 1st U.S. Infantry Division reorganized its brigades and battalions into task forces shortly after arriving in the area of operations north of Baghdad in March 2004. This was mainly accomplished by exchanging companies and cross-attaching platoons. In

the end, each task force is organized so it can conduct any type of mission that it might face within the theatre of operations.

During Operation "Iraqi Freedom 2," B Company of the 1-77 AR also includes the 2nd Platoon from C Company 9th Engineer Battalion "Gila Monsters" (with three M113A3s and one M1114 HWMMV); the 2nd Platoon from C Company, 1st Battalion, 18th Infantry Regiment "Vanguards" (with four M1114s); and the 3rd Platoon from D Company, 2nd Battalion, 108th Infantry Regiment "Hunters" from the New York Army National Guard (with four M1114s)

Normally, B Company "Regulators" of the 1-77 AR has 14 M1A1 AIM Abrams main battle tanks, but in Iraq only the two MBTs in the headquarters platoon remained, with the rest being cross-attached to other Task Forces of the 2nd "Dagger" Brigade Combat Team. Note the Combat Identification Panel attached to the side of the turret and the NBC overpressure system.

This combat patrol consisting of two M1A1 AIM Abrams and two M1114s was seen south of Balad at a crossroad near Highway 1. Despite the fielding of the M1A2, the M1A1 Abrams main battle tank remains the dominant ground combat platform in the Legacy Force. Today there are more than 1,000 M1A1s in active Armor and Cavalry units, and many more are in the reserve components and pre-positioned at locations around the globe. Because of a higher than normal mileage for the tanks during operations and training, the U.S. Army recognized the need to recapitalize the ageing M1A1 Abrams tanks.

TF 1-77 artillery support is provided by three 155mm M109A3 Paladin howitzers from the 1st Platoon, B Battery, 1st Battalion, 7th Field Artillery "First Lightning." The maximum firing range of the 155mm M284 cannon with the M182A1 cannon mount is 22 km (14 miles) with conventional artillery rounds. The range can be increased to 30 km (19 miles) through the use of Rocket Assisted Projectiles (RAP). The maximum rate of fire is four rounds per minute for three minutes. Afterwards, depending on the propelling charge, the sustained rate of fire is one round per minute for one hour.

The Battalion Task Force (TF) is the lowest echelon at which firepower, maneuver, intelligence, and other combined-arms support are combined under a single commander. Mechanized infantry and tank battalions are organized, equipped, and trained to accomplish compatible missions based on the respective battalion's unique capabilities and limitations. The tank and mechanized infantry battalions' capabilities are tailored through this task organization. Based on his estimate of the situation, the maneuver brigade commander task-organizes tank and mechanized infantry battalions by cross-attaching companies between units. Similarly, the Task Force commander's estimate may require cross-attaching platoons to form one or more company teams for specific missions.

The Task Force is formed by placing pure tank and mechanized infantry companies under the command of a battalion headquarters. Combat support (CS) and combat service support (CSS) elements within the brigade perform mission analysis and are integrated into the TF structure based on the higher commander's estimate of the mission and the assets required to accomplish the specific mission. This provides a versatile force mix, increasing the options available to the force commander. Each 1st ID Battalion Task Force has a different organization but normally they consist of a mix of armor, mechanized infantry, light infantry, artillery, and engineer platoons. Task Force 1-77 "Steel Tigers," which belongs to the 2nd Brigade Combat Team of the Big Red One, is responsible for the area around Balad and LSA Anaconda southwest of the 1st ID's area of operations. The Task Force is based on the 1st Battalion, 77th Armor Regiment stationed in the Logistic Supply Area (LSA) Anaconda and the Forward Operation Base (FOB) Paliwoda, both of which are located south of the city of Balad. Besides the Headquarters and Headquarters Company, TF 1-77 also includes B and C Company's 1-77 AR. A Company, 1-77 AR is cross-attached to TF 1-26 "Blue Spaders," but TF 1-77 received C Company from 1st Battalion, 26th Infantry Regiment equipped with the latest M2A2 ODS Bradley IFV.

The entire range of reorganization only becomes clearly visible if you take a close look on the Task Force at company level. Normally, B Company, 1-77 AR has 14 M1A1 AIM Abrams Main Battle Tanks, but in Iraq only the two MBTs in the headquarters platoon remained; the rest were cross-attached to other Task Forces of the 2nd BCT. During Operation "Iraqi Freedom 2," B Company, 1-77 AR also includes the 2nd Platoon from C Company, 9th Engineer Battalion "Gila Monsters" (with

The 26.1-ton M992A2 FAASV, based on the M109 chassis, is also powered by a 440 hp Detroit Diesel 8-cylinder, 8V71T diesel engine with turbocharger that provides a maximum speed of 56 km/h (35 mph). Vertical obstacles up to a height of 0.53 m (1.7 feet) and trenches up to a width of 1.83 m (6 feet) are no match for the M992A2 FAASV. The projectile rack assemblies and storage compartments have a capacity for 90 conventional rounds, three Copperhead rounds and 99 propelling charges.

Battalion medical support is provided by the medical platoon, which has a platoon headquarters with a HMMWV and a medical treatment squad with two M577A2 CPCs, two HMMWVs and two M101A1 cargo trailers. The medical treatment squad establishes a battalion aid station as far forward as possible, normally within the combat trains.

three M113A3s and one M1114 HWMMVs); the 2nd Platoon from C Company, 1st Battalion, 18th Infantry Regiment "Vanguards" (with four M1114s); and the 3rd Platoon from D Company, 2nd Battalion, 108th Infantry Regiment "Hunters" from the New York Army National Guard (with four M1114s). Other tank companies from TF 1-77 Armor have up to two infantry platoons from 1-26 INF, each equipped with four M2A2

ODS Bradleys. TF 1-77 artillery and mortar support is provided by three 155mm M109A3 Paladin howitzers from the 1st Platoon, B Battery, 1st Battalion, 7th Field Artillery "First Lightning" and four M1064A3 120mm mortars from the 1-77 AR organic mortar platoon. Both of these platoons are based in FOB Paliwoda and under the direct command of the task force commander, LTC David S. Hubner Sr.

Task Force 1-77 Organization

FOB Paliwoda

B Company 1-77 AR (Regulator)
HQ Plt, B Company 1-77 AR	(2x M1A1 AIM)
2nd Plt, C Company, 9 EN	(3x M113A3, 1x M1114)
2nd Plt, C Company, 1-18 INF	(4x M1114)
3rd Plt, D Company, 2-108 INF	(4x M1114)

C Company 1-26 IN (Rock)
1st Plt, C Company, 1-26 INF	(4x M2A2 ODS)
3rd Plt, C Company, 1-26 INF	(4x M2A2 ODS)
1st Plt, C Company ,1-77 AR	(4x M1A1 AIM)

HQ 1-77 Armor (2x M1A1 AIM)

Mortar Platoon	(4x M1064A3, 1x M577A2)
1st Plt, B Battery, 1 -7 FA	(3x M109A6)
CDR Personal Security Detachment	(4x M1114)
S3 Personal Security Detachment	(4x M1114)
TAC	(2x M577A2)

LSA Anaconda

C Company 1-77 AR (House of Pain)
HQ Plt, C Company, 1-77 AR	(3x M1114, 2x M113A3, 2x M998, 1x M88A1 , 1x M923)
3rd Plt, C Company, 1-77 AR	(4x M1114 , 2x M1A1 AIM)
2nd Plt, C Company, 1-26 INF	(2x M11114, 2x M113A3, 4x M2A2 ODS)

HHC 1-77 AR (Hellcat)
Scout Platoon 1-77 AR	(8x M1025/M1026)
2nd Platoon, B Company 2-108 INF	(4x M1114)

Field Trains

TOC	(2x M577A2)

This crew is ready to fire a 120mm M120 mortar to suppress the activity of Iraqi insurgents. The mortar platoon of the 1st Battalion, 77th Armor Regiment in FOB Paliwoda provides the indirect fire available to the TF 1-77 commander. Mortar units also fire smoke missions, mark targets and provide point battlefield illumination.

The mortar platoon is organized into a platoon headquarters with two HMMWVs and four mortar squads with 120mm M1064A3 mortar carriers and a mortar section with a M577A2 CPC that works as the Fire Direction Center (FDC) for the mortar squads.

This TF 1-77 mortar squad leader is equipped with the standard 5.56mm M4A1 carbine with an M68 sight. The M68 sight is a reflex sight that uses a red aiming reference (collimated dot) and is designed for the "two-eyes-open" method of sighting. The two-eyes-open method allows for quick acquisition of the target with a high hit probability.

Prioir to the deployment of the 1st Battalion, 77th Armor Regiment to Iraq, the Division planned to employ the soldiers in an infantry role, not as tankers with their heavy M1A1 AIM Abrams main battle tanks. Therefore, the unit was mostly equipped with up-armored M1114 HMMWVs when they left Conn Barracks in Schweinfurt, Germany, in January 2004. Only 16 M1A1 AIM were deployed for the OIF 2 mission, while the rest remained at home station. Because of the increasing violence and daily problems the 1st U.S. Infantry Division faced in Iraq, 28 additional M1A1 AIM tanks were immediately flown into the AO using C-17 Globemaster III cargo aircraft from 26 to 30 April 2004 to increase the firepower of the Division. Fourteen MBTs were quickly attached to the 2nd BCT, and the remaining 14 MBTs were attached to the 3rd BCT in the area around Baqubah in the eastern sector of the 1st ID AO. Currently, the "Steel Tigers" have 30 of their 44 M1A1 AIM Abrams, but only six are organized in TF 1-77.

The mission of TF 1-77 is to conduct offensive operations to defeat remaining non-compliant forces and neutralize destabilizing influences in their area of responsibility to create a secure environment in direct support of the new Iraqi government. In addition, the Task Force conducts stability operations that support the establishment of government and economic development to set conditions for a transfer of operations to designated follow-on military and civilian authorities.

A combat patrol of two M1114 HMMWVs leaves Forward Operating Base Paliwoda. The first vehicle is equipped with the 40mm Mk19 MOD 3 grenade machinegun, while the second one is armed with the reliable 50-cal. M2 machine gun. Note the Combat Identification Panels (CIP) and the front guard protecting the fiberglass components.

On May 2004, the U.S. Senate approved US$618 million for funding the production of 300 M1114s per month from May through October, and 450 per month from October 2004 to March 2006. $610 million were also allocated for armor kits for existing tactical vehicles. Note the tow bars attached to the rear of this B Company, 1-77 AR vehicle leaving FOB Paliwoda to conduct a combat patrol.

This soldier operates the new Force XXI Battle Command, Brigade-and-Below (FBCB 2) installed in a M1114 HMMWV. The FBCB2 provides situational awareness and command-and-control to the lowest tactical echelons. It facilitates a seamless flow of battle command information across the battle space and inter-operates with external command-and-control and sensor systems, such as ATCCS. The end result will be a vertical and horizontal integration of the digital battle space and the brigade-and-below tactical unit levels.

The FBCB 2 antenna is located behind the right launcher of the Light Vehicle Obscuration Smoke System (LVOSS). FBCB 2 will be one of the most significant digital tools for situational awareness for the Army. Using FBCB 2, a commander can look at a digital map on the computer display and see every vehicle in his brigade to 10-digit grid resolution. He can also transmit operations overlays with the push of a button instead of making copies and having liaison officers drive throughout the battlespace to deliver them hours later. Systems such as FBCB 2 are affording commanders and their staffs the freedom to focus on fighting rather than on mundane tasks to make the intelligence, command-and-control, communications, and fire processes work.

This Recon Section from C Company, 1-18 INF checks out a plantation east of Balad for any Iraqi insurgent activities and launch sites. Even when the situation looks very relaxed and quiet, the enemy could be everywhere in the overgrown fields and hedges. For many weeks, Forward Operating Base Paliwoda was attacked from this area with rockets and mortars that wounded and killed Big Red One soldiers.

Two TF 1-77 M113A3s leave FOB Paliwoda to transport two recon sections from C Company, 1st Battalion, 18th Infantry Regiment to the outskirts of Balad. Note the missing smoke grenade launchers and front plate. The armament consists only of one 7.62mm M240B machine gun attached to the commander's cupola.

Some M113A3s of the 9th Engineer Battalion received external stowage racks attached to the side of the APCs. The stowage racks were first used by the 54th Engineer Battalion based in Bamberg, Germany, who received them just days before the unit was deployed to Iraq in February 2004. Note the armor shield around the commander's station.

Specialist Edgar P. Daclan Jr. of Cypress, California, a member of the 1st Battalion, 18th Infantry, is armed with the 5.56mm M16A4 rifle with attached M68 reflex sight. The M16A4 rifle offers a performance identical to that of the M16A2. Physical differences between the two weapons include a removable carrying handle with an integral rail-mounting system on the M16A4. When the carrying handle is removed, any accessory device with a rail grabber, such as an optical sight, can be mounted on the weapon. Sadly, Specialist Daclan was killed 10 September 2004 by an IED as his patrol was responding to indirect fire in Balad, Iraq.

This recon soldier from Schweinfurt, Germany, relies on his 5.56mm M4A1 carbine with attached ACOG sight, flashlight and an AN/PEQ-2A aiming light. ACOG is an acronym for Advanced Combat Optical Gunsight, which is a four-power unit that uses both tritium and fiber-optic technology to illuminate the reticle. It is graduated out to a range of 800 meters (874 yards) with the 5.56mm cartridge. The red circle reticle covers four minutes-of-angle (MOA), with a hollow center that covers 2 MOA.

As the radio telephone operator, Specialist Carrier is responsible for the portable SINCGARS AN/PRC 119 multipurpose radio, which supports single-channel air-to-air, air-to-ground, and ground-to-air communications in tactical Navy and Marine Corps fixed- and rotary-wing aircraft. It can transmit and receive VHF-FM, VHF-AM, and UHF signals. It is compatible with SINCGARS, HAVE QUICK, and HAVE QUICK II frequency-hopping UHF radios, and it can accept 25 pre-set, single-channel frequencies.

Soldiers belonging to the 203rd Battalion of the Iraqi Civil Defense Corps (ICDC) were trained by members of the 5th Special Forces Group in Forward Operating Base Paliwoda. Note the chocolate-chip desert camouflage uniforms and the green load-bearing vests.

At the conclusion of the recon mission in a Named Area of Interest (NAI) in the plantation east of Balad, an M113A3 "battle taxi" waits to bring the three-man recon section back to FOB Paliwoda. Even though the GIs did not find any launch sites or Iraqi insurgents firing mortar, they will be back later that night for another reconnaissance patrol around the town to prevent the anti-Coalition forces from firing onto the FOB.

This much worn M2A2 ODS Bradley infantry fighting vehicle fitted with the new Explosive Reactive Armor is used as a spare-parts donor in FOB Paliwoda. Note the torsion bars, the shock absorbers and the new driver's hatch mount. There is also a cable cutter attached to the 25mm M242 main gun.

One of the many missions of TF 1-77 is route clearing along MSR Tampa and along the streets around Balad in the "Sunni Triangle." Route clearing operations are conducted more than once per day. Improvised Explosive Devices (IED) are the main threat to the U.S. supply convoys and patrols as they drive through Iraq. An IED can be almost anything, with any type of material and initiator. It is a homemade device that is designed to cause death or injury by using explosives alone or in combination with toxic chemicals, biological toxins, or radiological material. IEDs can be produced in varying sizes, functioning methods, containers, and delivery methods. IEDs can utilize commercial or military explosives, homemade explosives, or military ordnance and ordnance components.

Most IEDs are unique in nature because the builder has to improvise with the materials at hand. They are designed to defeat a specific target or type of target, so they generally become more difficult to detect and protect against as they become more sophisticated. IEDs share a common set of components: they consist of an initiation system or fuze, an explosive fill, a detonator, a power supply for the detonator, and a container. Many insurgents are using IEDs consisting of mortar and artillery projectiles as the explosive device. The use and characteristics of these have included the following:

- Thrown from overpasses.
- Thrown in front of approaching vehicles from roadside.
- Usually thrown by males (not always adults).
- Placed in potholes (covered with dirt).
- Placed along MSRs and alternate supply routes (targeting vehicles).
- Employed along unimproved roads (targeting patrols).
- Employed with 120mm and larger artillery or mortar projectiles.
- Found alone or in groups.
- IEDs behind which are placed cinder blocks or piles of sand to direct blast into the kill zone.
- Command-detonated, either by wire or remote device.
- Time-delay triggered IEDs. IEDs that can be detonated by cordless phone from a car (allows for mobile firing platform and prevents tracing or triangulation).

An M2A2 Bradley from C Company, 1st Battalion, 26th Infantry leaves LSA Anaconda on 1 June 2004 for a combat patrol south of Balad along Highway 1. To protect the Infantry Fighting Vehicles (IFV) against the rising threat from RPGs and IEDs, they were fitted with the new Explosive Reactive Armor (ERA) produced by General Dynamics Armament and Technical Products in co-operation with the RAFAEL Ordnance System Division in Israel.

On 1 June 2004 at around 0500h, the combat patrol of TF 1-77 – consisting of an M2A2 ODS Bradley, an M2A2 Bradley and two M1114 HMMWVs – discovered an Improvised Explosive Device on route Linda north of Yethrib. Immediately, the soldiers blocked the road to prevent civilians from getting injured by a possible IED explosion. Note the tow bar stowed on top of this IFV and the new exhaust system.

Depending on the mission and the threat level, the Task Force commander decides how many HMMWVs, Bradleys or Abrams he will send out on patrol to search for IEDs, establish Traffic Control Points, search for weapon caches, or observe a Named Area of Interest (NAI). But each patrol consists of at least four vehicles. Balad is ground zero for Ba'ath Party sentiment in Iraq. About 80% of the attacks against Coalition forces occur in this triangular area that is formed by Baghdad, Tikrit and Ar Ramadi. The paramilitary activity centers around the Tigris River between Baghdad and Samarra, more than 100 kilometers (61 miles) to the north. Balad falls right in the middle of that zone.

Sergeant Alvarez contacted a U.S. Air Force EOD team located in the Logistic Supply Area Anaconda with his AN/PRC-119 SINCGARS to help the TF 1-77 soldiers destroy the IED before it can injure soldiers or civilians. Note the Motorola ICOM radio and the pouches attached to his Interceptor Body Armor.

These soldiers from the 1st Battalion, 77th Armor Regiment "Steel Tigers" blocked and monitored the traffic while waiting for the Explosive Ordnance Disposal (EOD) team to arrive at the scene, which is located south of Balad. Some of Task Force 1-77's brand-new M1114 HMMWVs are painted in a sand color, while the majority of vehicles are still painted in the NATO three-color camouflage pattern. Each Big Red One soldier received a CamelBak hydration system that holds three liters of water, which is very helpful in the hot desert environment.

The first M2 Bradley IFVs entered service with the U.S. armored infantry in 1983. Designed for conventional warfare, in which large formations of armored vehicles fight each other using all available cover, the vehicle featured a welded armor of 5083 and 7039 aluminium combined with a steel, spaced laminate armor on parts of the hull. This armor offered the vehicle a basic protection against 14.5mm armor piercing rounds and splinters from 152mm high explosive shells. Note the cable cutters in front of the driver's hatch and the working platform below the turret.

The tiles of the M2A2 Explosive Reactive Armor, which look like small boxes, contain a special explosive charge that detonates when hit by a missile or rocket with a shaped-charge warhead. The resulting explosion disrupts the incoming, armor-penetrating gas jet produced by an RPG, for example, so the Bradley remains unharmed. The tiles are bolted onto rails that are screwed onto the mounting points of the steel appliqué armor. Fitting of the ERA kit is done on unit level, and a crew can fit the kit to their Bradley in less a day. Fitting is done with the tools available from the Bradley's tool kit and the tool kit of the battalions' maintenance element; no special tools are required.

Some soldiers of the Task Force 1-77 combat patrol are equipped with the new 5.56mm M16A4 rifle with attached M68 reflex sight. The soldier in the foreground attached the carrying handle on the integral rail mounting system. Note the magazine pouch attached to the butt stock and the gun shield for the 7.62mm M240B machine gun of the M1114 HMMWV.

A U.S. Air Force EOD team prepares a remote-controlled Vanguard robot for the destruction of an IED found on route Linda on 1 June 2004. The lightweight, portable, tactical EOD robot maintains excellence of quality with its additional features and improved functionality. It is transported by the M998 fitted with the ASK in the background.

This M1116 is used by the U.S. Air Force EOD team based in LSA Anaconda south of the city of Balad. Additional configuration details of the M1116 are an air-conditioning system, enlarged rear storage compartment, noise reduction kit, and a new heating system. Note the fence protecting the windshield and the Velcro attachment strips for the combat identification panels (CIP).

Improvised explosive devices, like this one that was found on route Linda on 1 June 2004, are produced in varying sizes, functioning methods, containers, and delivery methods. They can utilize commercial or military explosives, homemade explosives or military ordnance and ordnance components. The insurgents use the cable running from the IED to the shoulder of the street to detonate the device.

These three soldiers from C Company, 1st Battalion, 26th Infantry Regiment dismounted on route Linda south of Balad to monitor the shoulder and prevent Iraqi insurgents from attacking the EOD team while they destroy the IED that was placed on the morning of 1 June 2004. The dismounts are equipped with 5.56mm M16A4 rifles and a 5.56mm M249 Squad Automatic Weapon. Note the digital compass antenna attached to the right rear light, and the purple shine of the glass in the periscope.

The 25mm M242 main gun, TOW-2 missile launcher, and 7.62mm M240 machine gun provide adequate firepower to support the infantry while performing their missions in Iraq. The McDonnell Douglas M242 Bushmaster gun has a single barrel with an integrated dual-feed mechanism and remote ammunition selection. Either armor piercing (AP) or high explosive (HE) ammunition may be selected with the flick of a switch.

An M2A2 ODS Bradley from 1-26 INF monitors the shoulder of Route Amy while dismounts check a bridge for IEDs, mines or anything suspicious. The ERA kit was jointly developed, and is now produced, by General Dynamics Armament and Technical Products (USA) and RAFAEL (Israel). Development of the Bradley ERA began back in 1993, and the U.S. Army ordered an initial batch of 175 ERA kits in 1995. By 2004, the U.S. Army's TACOM/ARDEC had purchased 465 ERA kits, and another 170 partial sets were also purchased.

When facing heavier enemy armor, the Bradley relies on the TOW-2 anti-tank missile, which is manufactured by Hughes Aircraft. Launched from a smooth-tube launcher, the missile's wings and tail fins are folded inside its body until launch. Two of these missiles are carried in a ready-to-fire state in a collapsible, armored launch rack on the left side of the turret. The M2A2 ODS Bradley must stop in order to fire these missiles, which are then reloaded by infantrymen into the back of the vehicle, using a special hatch that provides armor protection during the reload operation.

A soldier belonging to the 1-26 INF uses an AN/PSS 12 mine detecting set to check a suspicious spot of Route Linda. It is designed to detect mines with very small proportions of metal content above ground and beneath the surface of fresh or salt water. Due to its compact, lightweight frame, the detector is ideal for fast and accurate terrain reconnaissance. The main technical features of the detector include excellent discrimination independent of ambient temperature and battery condition; sensitivity independent of search head speed; low mutual interference between two detectors; simple discrimination control; and built-in test circuit that automatically checks function and battery condition.

To protect the Coalition supply convoys from attacks from improvised explosive devices, the soldiers of Task Force 1-77 regularly check the bridges along route Linda, north of LSA Anaconda and Highway 1. The infantry soldiers are armed with 5.56mm M16A4 rifles with attached M68 reflex sights. Note the Wiley X ballistic glasses attached to the Kevlar combat helmet.

Two Bradley IFVs wait to transport soldiers back to LSA Anaconda after they finished checking a section of Route Amy south of Balad. The Bradley M2A2 ODS has been upgraded with improvements based on lessons learned during Operation "Desert Storm." These improvements include the following: an eye-safe laser rangefinder integrated with an upgraded turret drive-control system; navigation system integrating global positioning system/digital compass; improved electrical system; re-stowage of internal and external items, including MRE heater; bench seats in squad compartment; and mounting provisions for the Battlefield Combat Identification System (BCIS) and missile countermeasure device (MCD).

Besides a crew of three soldiers, the M2A2 ODS Bradley IFV can also transport seven fully equipped infantry soldiers. As part of the ODS program, the rear benches for the dismounted were improved and three 50-round 25mm ammunition ready boxes were installed in the floor. Because space is very limited inside the IFV, soldiers stow their personal equipment (like rucksacks and sleeping rolls) outside of the vehicle.

28 May 2004, 0330h A combat patrol from C Company, 1-77 AR prepares to leave LSA Anaconda with sixteen soldiers and four M1114 HMMWVs to clear Route Linda from the LSA to FOB Paliwoda and a section of Highway 1 southwest of Balad from IEDs and mines. The route clearance has to be accomplished by 0800h, before the first U.S. supply convoys arrive. The soldiers, who are armed with 5.56mm M4A1 carbines, 5.56mm M249 Squad Automatic Weapons and 7.62mm M240B machine guns, wear the new Interceptor Body Armor and the latest night vision goggles. It is 20°C (68°F) this morning, and they just performed the last checks on the four M1114s, loaded some additional boxes of water bottles onto the vehicles, and checked their weapons and radios. Even though the air-conditioning systems in the HMMWVs are running, the temperature inside each vehicle begins to rise, and sweat starts to run down the faces of the young soldiers who are normally based in Schweinfurt, Germany. To make matters worse, heat from the Detroit Diesel engines and the gearboxes is creeping into the crew compartment of the HMMWVs.

At 0400h, the awaited order to move out is given over the SINCGARS radios. The drivers change into gear D of the HMMWVs automatic transmission, and the combat patrol moves from the motor pool to the north gate. As they pass the gate, the GIs load and cock their weapons. The windows of the up-armored doors are open and the soldiers point their weapons outside. The air stream pushes into the vehicles, providing a little relief. The summer night is starlit, so the HMMWVs drive with only their blackout lights on so as to be invisible to Iraqi insurgents. The drivers find their way with the AN/PVS-14 and AN/PVS-7B night vision goggles that are clipped to their combat helmets.

The countryside is only illuminated by moonlight. Some kilometers outside of the LSA near the town Albu Shukur, the patrol stops as they recognize several civilian trucks driving through the night, even though there is a curfew from 2000h to 0600h. Albu Shukur is one of the hot spots in the AO of TF 1-77; several times it has been the origin of mortar and rockets attacks on LSA Anaconda. At 0425h the drivers switch on the lights of the HMMWV. By performing a left or right turn, the U.S. troops block the road, while the machine gunners aim their weapons at the approaching vehicles. Quickly the troops leave the HMMWVs and take up their position in a security perimeter. Armed with 5.56mm M4A1 carbines and 5.56mm M249 Squad Automatic Weapons, the soldiers quickly search the farmers' vehicles, which are loaded with baskets of fresh fruit and vegetables. It is market day, and the farmers want to transport their vegetables and fruits to the market in Balad. Of course, to do their best business, everyone wants to be the first at the market. After 30 minutes the search is finished, but nothing suspicious is found so the farmers are sent back home. But the checking of curfew violators is only one additional job for the patrol, whose main task is route clearing.

At around 0600h, the combat patrol of Sergeant First Class Eville stopped at the Police Station in Yethrib south of Balad, where the soldiers established a temporary Traffic Control Point (TCP), along with the Iraq National Police. Both M1114 HMMWVs are armed with 7.62mm M240B machine guns. Note the concrete wall protecting the police station against attacks by the Iraqi insurgents. The patrol came under attack at this location only two weeks earlier.

A young Iraqi translator (wearing an Interceptor Body Armor) supports the Task Force 1-77 soldiers while checking a car for illegal weapons and ammunition. Temporary control points are normally established for no longer than 30 minutes to prevent Iraqi insurgents from transmitting the information about the position to others, keeping them from getting checked. While some soldiers check the car, others check the passengers. Of course, only female U.S. soldiers check Iraqi females.

Shortly after leaving Yethrib, the combat patrol moves on to check a farmland area northwest of the police station from which insurgents have regularly launched rockets and mortar rounds on the LSA during the past weeks. Note the gun shield attached to the weapon station atop the HMMWV and the mounting of the rear mirror.

This gunner employed his .50-cal. M2 machine gun mounted on top of the M1114 HMMWV to provide security and monitor the traffic while the driver and the commanders searched the shoulder of Highway 1 for IEDs or anything suspicious. Note the spare wheel attached to the back and the Picatinny rail mount on top of the M2 that is used to attach a sight.

During the route clearance the lanes from Tikrit to Baghdad are completely closed by SFC Eville's combat patrol. Many Iraqis try to overtake or bypass the HMMWVs over dusty farm trails, but the soldiers prevent them from driving between the vehicles.

After one of the drivers identified a suspicious item (which turned out to be just a stinking trash bag filled with old fruit and vegetables), SFC Eville ordered his soldiers to dismount and check the shoulder of Highway 1 for possible IEDs. The M1114 HMMWVs provided security. Route clearance always has to be accomplished by 0800h, before the first U.S. supply convoys arrive.

From time to time, the TF 1-77 combat patrol stops to check suspicious cars, but this Iraqi farmer had nothing to hide; his truck was only loaded with some rusty oil barrels. The soldiers' armament consists of 5.56mm M4A1 carbines and 5.56mm M249 Squad Automatic Weapons. All soldiers of the 2nd "Dagger" Brigade have to wear knee and elbow protectors when on a mission off post.

While checking the shoulder of Highway 1, the soldiers always have to be aware of IEDs and mines. In some cases, IEDs have been placed along the road and hidden in dead animals. Most of the IEDs are unique in nature because the builder has to improvise with materials at hand. The soldier in front is armed with a 5.56mm M4A1 carbine with an ACOG sight, and he wears Wiley X ballistic glasses.

It is 0510h now and time for the combat patrol to move on. The next stop is at around 0600h at the police station in Yethrib south of Balad, where the soldiers establish a Traffic Control Point (TCP). Just like the sun climbing on the horizon, the temperature is also climbing, and it is now well above 30°C (86°F). The machine gunners in the weapon stations of the M1114s monitor the traffic with their machine guns at the ready. In the meantime, supported by an Iraqi translator and Iraqi National Police Officers, their comrades check some of the cars and trucks for illegal weapons and ammunition, but nothing is found today. Naturally, the very careful search for weapons at the TCP creates a long traffic jam. The farmers are very angry and nervous because they want to sell their goods, but the patrol leader (SFC Eville) has the situation under control.

For the troops, it is a daily routine to conduct vehicle searches. But it is also a daily routine to find nothing. Only two weeks earlier, the patrol came under attack at this location. A group of Iraqis armed with small arms and RPGs ambushed the patrol while the soldiers operated the TCP. The attack was followed by an intensive 30-minute gun battle. The attackers slipped away when the patrol received air support from AH-64D Apache combat helicopters and when reinforcements arrived. Luckily, no member of the patrol was badly injured. The final comment by the soldiers on the ambush is: "It's a shame we did not have our M1A1s down here during the attack, then we would have blasted them to hell."

After nearly one hour the combat patrol moves on to check an area northwest of the police station from which insurgents have regularly launched rockets and mortar rounds on the LSA over the past weeks. Here the situation remains quiet, and the patrol moves on to MSR Tampa to search for IEDs and mines that could have been put in place during the night to attack U.S. convoys. Highway 1 linking Baghdad with Mosul has four lanes, two in each direction, and each HMMWV of the combat patrol drives in one lane. The gunners, with their 7.62mm M240B machine guns mounted on top of the vehicles, provide security and monitor the traffic while the drivers and the commanders search the shoulder for IEDs or anything suspicious.

During route clearance, the lanes from Tikrit to Baghdad are completely closed by the combat patrol. Many Iraqis become nervous and honk their horns because they cannot overtake the patrol. Some of them try to use a detour, but the soldiers prevent them from driving between the HMMWVs of the combat patrol. The Iraqis do not understand that this mission is very dangerous and they risk their lives by trying to drive between the HMMWVs. The cars and trucks on the way from Baghdad to Tikrit have to drive in wavy lines through the two HMMWVs on their lanes heading against the direction of the traffic. To prevent a crash, all vehicles of the patrol drive with warning lights. But sometimes the Iraqi drivers change the lanes at the very last second or just stop in front of the patrol vehicles, driving the soldiers crazy. It is a wonder that nobody has been injured so far.

After one of the drivers identifies a suspicious item on the shoulder, SFC Eville orders his soldiers to dismount and check it from a safe distance. It was only a stinking, gray trash bag filled with old fruit and vegetables, and the soldiers kick it into the field and go on with the patrol

After finishing the route clearance along Highway 1, the soldiers of the TF 1-77 combat patrol check an area consisting of farmland, located west of the Highway, from which Iraqi insurgents have regularly launched rockets and mortar round on LSA Anaconda. Note the M68 reflex sight, the AN/PEQ-2A aiming light and the flashlight mounted on the 5.56mm M4A1 carbine.

Sergeant Wallat from the 1st Battalion, 77th Armor Regiment is armed with a Remington 12-gauge pump shotgun. Note both the Motorola ICOM radio attached to his Interceptor Body Armor and his black fingerless gloves.

Like his soldiers, Sergeant First Class Eville is also normally based at Conn Barracks in Schweinfurt, Germany. He is armed with a 5.56mm M4A1 carbine with an attached M68 reflex sight, AN/PEQ-2A aiming light and a flashlight. Note the Magellan GPS and the ammunition pouches attached to his Interceptor Body Armor, as well as his ballistic glasses.

up to a crossroad southwest of FOB O'Ryan. In the past, IEDs have sometimes been placed along the road, and even hidden in dead animals. It is 0900h and the temperature has climbed to 40°C (104°F), but the patrol still has to conduct some more missions today. For the next two hours the soldiers check an area consisting of farmland west of Highway 1 from which Iraqi insurgents regularly launched rockets and mortar rounds on the LSA. The 57mm, 81mm and 107mm rockets, and the 82mm and 60mm mortar rounds, are the main threat to the soldiers in the large logistic supply area. Unfortunately, conversations with the local farmers and kids elicit no new information about Iraqi insurgents operating in this area and terrorizing U.S. soldiers. By now, the soldiers' CamelBak hydration systems, which contain three liters of water, are nearly empty and water bottles are handed around to refill them.

On the way back to the LSA, the patrol stops beside a bridge crossing MSR Tampa. Just after the soldiers arrive, a couple of kids from a nearby building approach the soldiers. The soldiers give them some candy, as well

as some small plastic toys, and within a couple of minutes the ice between the children and the GIs is broken. Smiles appear on the faces of the young kids when they receive the candy. From a distance the parents watch their children, but neither the soldiers nor the parents make an attempt to get in touch. The soldiers managed to win the hearts and minds of the kids but the gap between the U.S. troops and the older Iraqis would remain unbridged until another day.

Around 1200h the patrol returns to LSA Anaconda. At the main gate the daily chaos is in progress with hundreds of local trucks wanting to deliver goods to the base. Each has to be checked by the guards, which include U.S. soldiers and ICDC personnel. The approach road is nearly blocked and it takes SFC Eville and his men time to maneuver their trucks through the traffic to the gate. In front of the gate, the soldiers unload their weapons and conduct safety checks. After the troops have parked their vehicles in the motor pool, the soldiers have time to get lunch in one of the four huge air-conditioned dining facilities operated by the U.S. contractor ESS. The food is delicious and the soldiers from Schweinfurt, Germany, can choose between various meals and drinks, but they will only have a very short break. After lunch they will have to clean their weapons and check their equipment because they will be conducting the next combat patrol at 1700h and remain on patrol until 2330h.

Besides route clearing operations, the missions of TF 1-77 also include joint patrols and raids with the 203rd Iraqi Civil Defense Corps (ICDC) Battalion. The 203rd ICDC Battalion, which consists of a headquarters and headquarters company and four line companies, is based in the area around Balad. In April 2004, after receiving information from local citizens, TF 1-77 and ICDC soldiers conducted numerous raids west of Balad and took out several cells of Iraqi insurgents, one of them consisting of 12 people. Sometimes, TF 1-77 soldiers also set up Observation Points (OP) in a Named Area of Interest (NAI) from which anti-coalition forces have fired rockets and mortars into the camps, or where many IEDs have been placed. Another of the many missions of the Task Force is escorting civilian fuel convoys from FOB Speicher, located east of Tikrit, to the LSA. Last but not least, the soldiers search for weapons and ammunition caches and conduct cordon-and-search operations in their area of responsibility.

Before the soldiers of the TF 1-77 soldiers check the farmland for possible rocket launch sites, SFC Eville holds a short briefing. The 57mm, 81mm and 107mm rockets, and the 82mm and 60mm mortar rounds, are the main threat to the soldiers and civilian contractors in the large logistic supply area south of Balad. Note the mounts for the night vision goggles attached to the Kevlar helmets.

On the way back to the LSA, the patrol stops beside a bridge crossing MSR Tampa. Note the Combat Identification Panels attached to the front and side of this M1114 HMMWV and the armor shield for the M240B machine gun. Most of the TF 1-77 HMMWVs are still painted in the NATO camouflage pattern, not in the desert sand color.

SGT Schulz is equipped with the vintage M21 sniper rifle, which was officially type classified as M21 in 1975. It was the primary Army sniper rifle of the Vietnam War and remained standard until replaced by the bolt-action M24 Sniper Weapon System beginning in 1988. The M21, which is accurate to 690m (750 yards), uses U.S. match grade M118 NATO 7.62mm cartridges in five-round or 20-round magazines. The ART telescope features a variable magnification power of from 3X to 9X for adjustable ranging between 300m and 900m (328 and 984 yards).

Prior to the deployment of the 1st Battalion, 77th Armor Regiment to Iraq, the 1st U.S. Infantry Division planned to employ the soldiers in an infantry role, not as tankers with their heavy M1A1 AIM Abrams main battle tanks. Therefore, the unit was mostly equipped with up-armored M1114 HMMWVs when they left Conn Barracks in Schweinfurt, Germany, in January 2004.

Private Chumbiriza provided cover while his comrades searched for the rocket launch sites next to MSR Tampa. Most of the TF 1-77 soldiers use the RIS-mounted forward handgrip, M68 reflex sights and AN/PEQ-2A aiming lights, but only a few also added flashlights to their weapons. The M4A1 is a lightweight, gas-operated, air-cooled, magazine-fed, selective-rate, shoulder-fired weapon with a collapsible stock. A shortened variant of the M16A2 rifle, the M4A1 provides the individual soldier operating in close quarters the capability to engage targets at extended range with accurate, lethal fire. Note his knee and elbow protectors and the DCU scarf covering his face.

"Winning Hearts and Minds." Just after the arrival of the combat patrol, a couple of kids from a nearby building approach the soldiers. Sergeant Sloma gives them some candy, as well as some small plastic toys, and within a couple of minutes the ice between the children and the GI is broken.

29 May 2004, 0300h The night is very quiet and starlit when the soldiers of HHC and C Company, 1-77 AR and B Company, 2-108th INF leave LSA Anaconda through the north gate for Operation "Rocket Man 2." All HMMWVs and two M2A2 ODS Bradley IFVs drive with blackout lights to prevent the anti-Coalition forces from identifying the position of the convoy while they are on the way to accomplish their mission. Tonight, as usual, the soldiers check the shoulders for any suspicious items or possible IEDs. Like so often in the past months, the U.S. soldiers own the night thanks to their very advanced and effective night vision equipment. Today they will search for illegal weapons and ammunition caches beside the Tigris River close to the town of Albu Shukur.

The tactics of the insurgents are always the same: they put the rockets in steel pipes, which they ram into the ground and aim in the direction of the LSA. Depending on the aiming skills of the insurgents, the rockets hit the LSA or just fly over the huge base. They mostly use time fuzes made of alarm clocks to ignite the rockets since they are difficult for the Coalition forces to trace. Just seconds after rockets or mortars are fired, the AN/TPQ-36(V)8 and AN/TPQ-37(V)8 Firefinder radar of the 1st Battalion, 33rd Field Artillery MLRS/TA "Golden Lions" based in the LSA Anaconda locate the point of origin and send the co-ordinates forward to TF 1-77 artillery and mortar teams for immediate counterfire missions. For many weeks, both day and night, the soldiers of the 2nd Battalion, 108th Infantry Regiment (based in LSA Anaconda and FOB O'Ryan) conducted numerous reconnaissance patrols around the town and close by

the river without catching the insurgents in the act. Establishing observation points in the NAI did not help them to successfully catch the insurgents, either.

Now, after a 48-hour planning period, over 150 U.S. troops have sealed the region and will conduct a search for possible rocket-launch sights and weapons caches. Led by TF 1-77, "Rocket Man 2" involves troops from the 1st Battalion, 77th Armor Regiment; 2nd Battalion, 108th Infantry Regiment and the 1st Battalion, 26th Infantry Regiment. Between 0400h and 0600h, under the over of darkness, the troops move into position and seal the area around Albu Shukur. After all soldiers and

The soldiers of the New York Army National Guard use the same equipment, weapons and uniforms as their regular Army counterparts. This soldier from the 1st Platoon of B Company, 2-108th INF opens a shed's locked metal door with his 12-gauge Remington pump shotgun to search for caches. His secondary armament consists of a 5.56mm M4A1 carbine.

Soldiers of B Company, 2nd Battalion, 108th Infantry Regiment (belonging to the New York Army National Guard) open a very ordinary looking shed beside the Tigris River to search for weapons and ammunition caches. Like their Regular Army comrades, all ANG soldiers in Iraq wear the Interceptor Body Armor, as well as the new 1.4-kg Advanced Combat Helmets.

Each of the rifle squads has a squad leader and two teams consisting of a team leader, an automatic rifleman, a grenadier, and a rifleman. The rifle platoon's armament consists of five 5.56mm M4A1 carbines, two M4A1 carbines with M203A1 40mm grenade launchers, and two 5.56mm M249 Squad Automatic Weapons.

After opening a shed beside the riverbanks of the Tigris, this NYANG soldier did not find any weapons, but some capacitors and electrical components were confiscated to prevent Iraqi insurgents from using them for improvised explosive devices. Note the engine-driven water pump used to irrigate the field and plantations.

These two NYANG soldiers use an AN/PSS-12 mine detector and a shovel to search for hidden IEDs and weapons during Operation "Rocket Man 2." Metal detectors are frequently described as being either of the pulse induction (PI) or continuous wave (CW) type, with the AN/PSS-12 belonging to the former category. The AN/PSS-12 search head uses two concentric coils; the outer is used to transmit and the inner to receive. An electric current driven through the transmitter coil causes a magnetic field to penetrate any metallic object near the search head. When the transmitter current is abruptly extinguished, eddy currents are induced into nearby metallic objects in accordance with Faraday's Law of induction. As the eddy currents decay, they radiate a secondary or scattered magnetic field that induces a voltage into the receiver coil. This voltage is amplified and is used to detect the presence of a metallic object. The AN/PSS-12 makes a clicking sound while operating rather than remaining silent.

Today's aerial support is provided by AH-64D Apache attack helicopters and scouts with their OH-58D (I) Kiowa Warriors from the 1st Cavalry Division. They hover over the trees and look for anything suspicious in front of the soldiers.

The 2nd Battalion, 108th Infantry Regiment, with its headquarters and headquarters company, three rifle companies and an anti-armor company, is an air assault unit belonging to the New York Army National Guard, which was attached to the 1st ID, 2nd Brigade Combat Team for Operation "Iraqi Freedom 2." Today, Army National Guard units are trained and equipped like active Army units, but they have two missions: they can be activated by their state for state emergencies or federalized and deployed by the national government. Under Federal law, the Army cannot police the citizens of the United States. Consequently, only National Guard units can be utilized for civil assistance within the USA. Federal law also mandates that any National Guard soldier who is mobilized must be guaranteed his job upon return – with the exact same benefits and opportunities as if he had remained on the job the whole time. Problems arise when the Guardsmen are employed by local community agencies, for example, police department, fire department, paramedics, and governmental authorities. Naturally, gaps here can hardly be closed for a period of several years and the man is just missing. In some cases, this fact worries the Guardsmen since their civilian jobs are equally as important as their Army Reserve jobs. But even with these things in mind, active and reserve troops also have strong similarities, including a professional attitude, unit cohesion and sense of mission.

Like the other rifle platoons of the 2nd Battalion, 108th Infantry Regiment, 1st Platoon, which is led by 1LT Tabankin, has a platoon headquarters, three rifle squads and a weapons squad. Each of the rifle squads has a squad leader and two teams that consist of a team leader, an automatic rifleman, a grenadier, and a rifleman. The rifle platoon's armament consists of five 5.56mm M4A1 carbines, two M4A1 carbines with M203A1 40mm grenade launchers, and two 5.56mm M249 Squad Automatic Weapons. There are two 7.62mm M240B machine-gun teams and two Javelin anti-armor teams in the weapons squad that provide the platoon with tripod-supported machine gun and anti-armor fire.

Because the plantations and fields are nearly 15 meters higher than the water level of the Tigris River, the farmers use diesel-engine-driven

While an AH-64D Apache from the 1st Cavalry Division hovers over the reeds of the Tigris River banks, this Army National Guard soldier checks his position with a Magellan GPS receiver. The standard weapon used by the soldiers of the 2nd Battalion, 108th Infantry Regiment is the 5.56mm M4A1 carbine.

vehicles are in position for today's operation, the search begins with the sunrise at around 0630h northwest of the town at Phaseline Audi. It is 25°C (77°F) this morning.

From the line of departure, each deployed platoon starts to move down its assigned strip of landscape. Today, the 1st Platoon of B Company, 2-108th INF has the task of clearing the first 200-300 meters (219-328 yards) south of the Tigris River of any weapons or ammunition caches in order to deny the enemy their use. The platoon leader, First Lieutenant Tabankin, received the operation orders two days earlier to plan his mission. South of his platoon is the scout platoon of HHC, 1-77 AR. C Company, 1-77 AR is tasked with searching in the town Albu Shukur. Because of the many hedges, fields and fruit plantations, it is very difficult for the soldiers to find the caches or launch sights.

Advancing in an extended line, the soldiers of the New York Army National Guard make their way down the river bank, moving through the thick undergrowth of palm trees. Communication between the Task Force headquarters, the companies, the platoons, and the teams is a key element in this kind of terrain to co-ordinate the movement from one checkpoint to the next. Every 500 meters (547 yards), the deployed platoons stop to make sure they are still in one line. From time to time the soldiers use AN/PSS 12 mine detectors to search pre-selected locations. Each platoon was given up to eight such locations, which could be a particular field or a fruit orchard. The temperature is around 47°C (116°F), but each soldier continues to wear the 8-kg (18-lb) Interceptor Body Armor and the new 1.4-kg (2.4-lb) Advanced Combat Helmet for protection against small arms fire and artillery shrapnel. By now the soldiers are very happy that they were issued CamelBaks hydration systems.

Aerial support during Operation "Rocket Man 2" was provided by AH-64D Apache attack helicopters and scouts with their OH-58D (I) Kiowa Warriors from the 1st Cavalry Division. Hovering over the trees and plantations, they looked for anything suspicious in close proximity to the soldiers. It feels very good feeling to know the pilots are maintaining a watchful eye and are searching for Iraqi insurgents hiding in the plantations.

Communication between the Task Force headquarters, the companies, the platoons, and the teams is a key element in co-ordinating the movement from one checkpoint to the next in this type of terrain. Every 500 meters the deployed platoons stop to make sure they are still in one line. This Radio Telephone Operator (RTO) uses an AN/PRC-119 SINCGARS radio.

Today, Army National Guard units are trained and equipped like active Army units, but they have two missions – they can be activated by their state for state emergencies or federalized and deployed by the national government. Under Federal law, the Army cannot be used to police the citizens of the United States, so only National Guard units can be used for civil assistance in the USA. Note 1LT Tabankin's radio headset attached to his Advanced Combat Helmet.

water pumps stowed in small sheds beside the cliff for irrigation. Since the soldiers expect the sheds to be used as weapon and ammunition caches, they open the locks with cutters (and sometimes with pump shotguns). A loud bang breaks the silence of the Tigris River Valley when a soldier from B Company, 2nd Battalion, 108th Infantry Regiment uses his 12-gauge pump shotgun to open the looked door of a pump house on the river bank. With one shot the lock of the door is breached, and two guardsmen quickly enter the building. After they troops have made sure that nobody is hiding in the building, they search for weapons . . . but nothing is found. Every time the National Guardsmen pass one of the given phase lines (which are called Audi, Volvo, Porsche, and Mercedes), they report their progress to the higher command. The temperature continues to rise, and soon the search operation becomes a boring, hot business. After the soldiers search the riverbanks to a length of five kilometers (3 miles), their day's mission is accomplished. They are happy to re-deploy to their HMMWVs waiting in the town of Albu Shukur around 1400h to be taken back to the LSA. Even though the GIs did not find any weapons or ammunition this day, they will be back at night for another reconnaissance patrol around the town to prevent the anti-Coalition forces from firing on LSA Anaconda.

Because the NYANG soldiers expect that the water-pump sheds will be used as weapons and ammunition caches, they open the locks with cutters and even with pump shotguns. Note the plastic handcuffs and the CamelBak hydration system attached to the Interceptor Body Armor.

Using a handheld Motorola ICOM radio, Staff Sergeant Derocher co-ordinates the movement of a squad. Note how he affixed the M4A1 carbine's sling to the Interceptor Body Armor. Many soldiers received Wiley X ballistic glasses before they deployed to Iraq.

This gunner of the 2-108 INF is armed with the shorter paratrooper version of the 5.56mm M249 SAW. The main difference from the standard version is the telescoped butt stock and the shorter barrel. The M249 SAW is an air-cooled, gas-operated, belt-fed, automatic weapon. The SAW is operated using conventional gas action with the gas piston located below the barrel, and the barrel is locked using the traditional rotary bolt. The barrel is quickly detachable and has a carrying handle attached to it for swift replacement. It has an alternative feed system, which allows for using disintegrating metallic belts as a primary feed option or M16-type box magazines as a backup feed option.

Led by TF 1-77, "Rocket Man 2" involved troops from the 1st Battalion, 77th Armor Regiment; 2nd Battalion, 108th Infantry Regiment; and the 1st Battalion, 26th Infantry Regiment. This soldier belongs to the Headquarters and Headquarters Company of the 1st Battalion, 77th Armor Regiment.

A soldier from HHC, 1-77 Armor searches a field with an AN/PSS-12 detector. The AN/PSS-12 mine detector replaces the PSS-11 Metallic Mine Detector. The PSS-11 had reached its end of service life and needed to be replaced with state-of-the-art technology. The AN/PSS-12 represents a world-class mine detector capable of detecting the small amounts of metal found in modern land mines.

After having accomplished the search for weapons and ammunitions caches, these soldiers of Bravo Company, 2-108 INF walk through the village of Albu Shukur. Like the other rifle platoons of the 2-108 INF, 1st Platoon (led by 1LT Tabankin) also has a platoon headquarters, three rifle squads and a weapons squad.

Taking part in Operation "Rocket Man 2," this soldier is equipped with a pump shotgun and a 5.56mm M4A1 carbine. Note the mount for the Night Vision Goggles and the Wiley X ballistic glasses attached to his Advanced Combat Helmet. The M4A1 has an attached AN/PEQ-2A aiming light and a forward handgrip.

Each rifle team includes an automatic rifleman equipped with a 5.56mm M249 Squad Automatic Weapon. Note the woodland-pattern camouflage ammunition bag attached to this paratrooper SAW version, which has a shorter barrel than the standard version.

After finishing their mission, the soldiers of Task Force 1-77 re-deployed to LSA Anaconda on some HMMWVs that were already waiting in Albu Shukur. During Operation "Iraqi Freedom 2," the Headquarters and Headquarters Company of the 1st Battalion, 77th Armor Regiment is also equipped with three M1114 HMMWVs to provide mobility.

The GIs are very inventive in protecting themselves against the Iraqi insurgents. This regular M998 HMMWV received not only the new Armor Survivability Kit (ASK) but also a 7.62mm M240B machine gun with a mount fixed to the floor of the cargo compartment. Note the custom-made armor around the cargo compartment, which should protect the gunner from small arms fire.

This M1026 HMMWV is fitted with a prototype version of the new Armor Survivability Kit (ASK) in order to protect the vehicle crew against attacks with IEDs, RPGs and small arms fire. As of the time of writing, some 8,000 of the 12,000 HMMWVs used in Iraq are fitted with the ASK kits. The ballistic door windows can be opened to enable the soldiers to fire their weapons from inside the vehicle. Note the new ballistic windshield and the front winch.

Some of the M1114 HMMWVs are equipped with the Light Vehicle Obscuration Smoke System (LVOSS). The LVOSS, which counters the threat of weapon systems operating in the visual and near infrared portion of the electromagnetic spectrum, has a push-button Arming/Firing Unit (A/FU) that allows the operator to select the direction he needs obscured. Additionally, the LVOSS uses smoke grenades that are low in toxicity and which minimize safety hazards to personnel and the environment

This 155mm M109A6 Paladin howitzer belonging to Task Force 1-7 was photographed during live firing at FOB Summerall near Bayji in June 2004. The Paladin/FAASV Howitzer Improvement Program (HIP), which began 1985, is the third and most extensive modernization of the M109 series, whose technology dates back to the 1950s. Range, lethality, reliability, speed, and mobility were all limitations of this 1950s design, as was the lack of onboard navigation/location and nuclear, biological and chemical protection for the crew

Each M270 SPLL holds either two Launch Pods Containers (LP/C) with six rockets each or two Guided Missile Launch Assemblies (GMLA) with one ATACM each. This crew from the 1st Battalion, 33rd Field Artillery "Golden Lions" reloads the M270 with LP/Cs during a mission in FOB Summerall. One crewman holds the boom controller that permits remote loading and off-loading functions while the other holds the LP/C.

Task Force 1-7 spent February 2004 preparing for combat and deploying for Operation "Iraqi Freedom 2." The first element of TF Lightning – LTC McClelland and CPT Emmel – departed by air on 4 February in order to provide command and control for the entire division at the Aerial Port of Debarkation (APOD) in Kuwait. TF 1-7 soldiers arrived with more than 15,000 of the Big Red One and 30th ESB in Kuwait and coordinated their movement to their base camps of Camp Udairi and Camp New York, located in the northern deserts of the country. The remainder of the Task Force deployed on 11 February from Ledward Barracks in Schweinfurt, Germany, and began last minute preparations for the movement north into their sector in Bayji, Iraq, their home for the next twelve months. Additionally, the 1st Battalion, 7th Field Artillery "First Lightning" organized into what would be known as Task Force 1-7, detaching platoons from B Battery, 1-7 FA to the 9th Engineer Battalion in FOB Remagen and Task Force 1-77 in FOB Paliwoda.

To accomplish its mission during OIF 2, Task Force 1-7 gained attachments of 1st Platoon, A Company, 1-26 INF; 1st Platoon, B Company, 1-18 INF; 9th Engineer Battalion; C Company, 201st ICDC Battalion; a Maintenance Support Team from Task Force 299th FSB; a team from the 115th Signal Battalion; and Team 2 from A Company, 415th Civil Affairs Battalion. E Troop, 4th Cavalry (the 2nd Brigade reconnaissance organic element) was attached to TF Lightning from 15 April to 20 July 2004. The troop was supported with a tank section from the 1st Battalion, 77th Armor Regiment and a mortar section from B Troop, 1st Squadron, 4th U.S. Cavalry. Tank sections were rotated to support maintenance and crew rotations, as well as to allow the time- and labor-intensive annual services to occur to allow them to maintain optimal readiness. B Troop, 1st Squadron, 4th U.S. Cavalry does not habitually belong to Task Force 1-7 but was sent to FOB Summerall on a temporary basis by the Division Commander, Major General Batiste. The Bulldog troop is composed of two M3A2 ODS Bradley-equipped scout platoons, two M1A1 AIM Abrams tank platoons and an M1064A3 120mm mortar section. The attachment of such elements is what makes Task Force 1-7 so unique, instead of being merely 1-7 Field Artillery.

The M26 rocket is the basic rocket for the MLRS, which can attack targets at ranges between 10 to 32 km (6.2 to 20 miles). It is a tube-launched, fin-stabilized, free-flight projectile that is assembled, inspected and packaged in a dual-purpose launch-storage tube at the factory. This design provides for tactical loading and firing of the rocket without troop assembly or detailed inspection. The rockets can be fired individually or in ripples of two to twelve. Accuracy is maintained in all firing modes because the computer re-aims the launcher between rounds.

The water-cooled Cummins VTA-903T V8 diesel engine with turbocharger and 14.8-liter displacement provides 506 gross horsepower. It is connected to a General Electric HMPT-500-3EC automatic transmission with hydrostatic steering and multi-disc, oil-cooled brakes.

The M93A1 Fox NBCRS is a rolling laboratory that takes air, water and ground samples and immediately analyzes them for signs of weapons of mass destruction. It is intended to improve the survivability and mobility of the Army ground forces by providing increased situational awareness and information superiority to headquarters and combat maneuver elements. With the ability to provide rapid, accurate chemical and radiological contamination information to these elements, the NBCRS vehicle forms a key portion of the full-dimensional protection concept.

During Operation "Iraqi Freedom 2," the 12th Chemical Company "Hellfire" is attached to Task Force 1-33 (based in Forward Operation Base Summerall). One of the major differences between the M93 and the M93A1 Fox NBCRS is the reduced crew, which now consists of the commander, the driver and only one operator. The M21 RSCAAL is now fitted on the roof on a mount that allows 180° rotation and levelling in all three axes. The new meteorological sensor measures wind speed, direction, air and ground temperature, and relative humidity while the vehicle is stopped.

Final preparations included drawing new gear under the Rapid Fielding Initiative, Convoy Live Fire Exercise, Close Quarter Battles/Marksmanship training, Equipment Reception at the Seaport of Debarkation (SPOD) in Kuwait, equipment preparations for movement, and finally, the Tactical Approach March into Iraq. After three days of road marching from Kuwait to Iraq, TF Lightning arrived at FOB Lancer near Bayji on 6 March 2004. They were greeted with a warm welcome by TF 3-66 (Lancer), 1st BCT, 4th U.S. Infantry Division, from Fort Hood, Texas. After a brief rest from the long approach march, the TF began a battle handover/relief-in-place with Task Force 3-66, riding along and learning lessons that the Lancers had learned over the past year in sector. After learning as much as they could from the soldiers of TF Lancer, TF Lightning took control of the area of operation (AO) in the battle-handover ceremony on 15 March 2004. The FOB was renamed on 16 March 2004 after the 1st ID assumed the mission of 4th ID; it was named after General Charles P. Summerall, the WWI commander of the 1st Infantry Division, former Chief of Staff of the Army and winner of the Congressional Medal of Honor.

The mission of Task Force 1-7 is to conduct combat operations in AO Lightning to neutralize or capture non-compliant forces in order to establish a stable and secure environment and, simultaneously, to conduct stability operations to gain the support of the local populace and enable the transition to designated Iraqi authorities and/or follow-on forces in preparation for Iraqi self-reliance. In addition to assisting with the emplacement of a local government, the Task Force helps train and equip the new Iraqi Police Service and Iraqi National Guard (formerly known as the Iraqi Civil Defense Corps [ICDC]). The Task Force also assists with the funding, management and construction of such projects as water projects, schools, police stations, and medical clinics.

Task Force Lightning was charged with many tasks that occurred on a daily basis, and although none of these ever seemed routine, they became part of the daily missions that were essential to operations within the AOs of the Task Force, 2nd Brigade Combat Teams and the 1st Infantry Division. One of the most important tasks for Task Force 1-7, as well as for all of the Multinational Force-Iraq area, was route clearance of Highway 1. This consists of deliberately clearing the highway of mines, IEDs and any anti-Coalition forces. TF 1-7 also executed and supervised traffic control points along Highway 1 that were primarily run by the Iraqi Civil Defense Corps and Iraqi National Police. Also included in the daily operations were combat patrols that ensured the safety of key

infrastructure in Bayji and Ash Sharqat area, specifically the northern oil refinery, the Bayji fertilizer plant, the thermal power plant, the Al-Fatah bridge construction site, and the 400KV power lines. One of the most tedious daily tasks was combat logistics patrols (CLPs), which entailed driving south along Highway 1 towards Tikrit to FOB Speicher in order to draw necessary supplies for the daily operations at FOB Summerall. As is obvious, soldiers of TF 1-7 are primarily used in an infantry, not an artillery role.

The 12.8-liter 320hp liquid-cooled Daimler-Benz OM 402A 8-cylinder Diesel engine with two turbochargers provides the 18.7-ton vehicle a maximum speed of up to 105km/h (65mph). The two self-sealing rubber fuel tanks have a capacity of 390 liters (103 gallons), providing a cruising range of up to 797km (495 miles). The M93 Fox NBCRS, which is fully amphibious, can achieve a maximum speed of over 10km/h (6.2mph) in the water by using the two rudder propellers installed at the rear of the vehicle. The armament consists of a 7.62mm M240 machine gun, four 5.56mm M16A2s, four AT-4s, eight M67 hand grenades, and two M250 smoke launchers.

Task Force 1-7 Organization

FOB Summerall

A Battery, 1-7 FA (Steel Knight)
HQ Plt, A Battery, 1-7 FA
1st Plt, A Battery, 1-7 FA
2nd Plt, A Battery, 1-7 FA
3rd Plt, A Battery, 1-7 FA
CSE
1st Plt, B Company, 1-18 INF

C Battery, 1-7 FA (Cobra)
HQ Plt, C Battery, 1-7 FA
1st Plt, C Battery, 1-7 FA
2nd Plt, C Battery, 1-7 FA
3rd Plt, C Battery, 1-7 FA
1st Plt, A Company, 1-26 INF
HQ Plt, A Company, 1-77 AR
1st Plt, C Company, 201 IDCD

B Troop, 1-4 CAV (Bulldog)
HQ Plt, B Troop, 1-4 CAV
1st Plt, B Troop, 1-4 CAV
2nd Plt, B Troop, 1-4 CAV
3rd Plt, B Troop, 1-4 CAV
4th Plt, B Troop, 1-4 CAV
SCT Plt, B Troop, 1-4 CAV
3rd Plt, C Company, 201 ICDC

HHB 1-7 FA (Hurricane)
HHB, 1-7 FA
2nd Plt, C Company, 201 ICDC
4th Plt, C Company, 201 ICDC

SVC 1-7 FA (Serpent)
SVC Battery, 1-7 FA
MST 299th FSB

1st Plt, A Company, 9 EN
Team 115 SIG BN
Mortar Section, 1-18 INF
Team 2, A Company, 415th Civil Affairs Battalion

FOB Tinderbox

E Troop, 4 CAV (Renegade) from 15 April to 20 July 2004
HQ Plt, E Troop, 4 CAV
2nd Plt, E Troop, 4 CAV
COLT, E Troop, 4 CAV
Mortar Section, B Troop, 1-4 CAV
One tank section from 1-77

Task Force Lightning spent a significant amount of time, effort and thought rebuilding a defeated and unorganized Iraq into a nation that could be proud of its accomplishments and diverse heritage. Lifetimes of memories and lifelong friendships have developed amongst the varied backgrounds and dreams of local Iraqi leaders and the leaders of TF 1-7. On 8 May 2004, TF 1-7 conducted a ribbon-cutting ceremony that marked the opening of the new C Company Headquarters of the 201st ICDC Battalion. On 26 May 2004, TF 1-7 conducted a ground-breaking ceremony that marked the beginning of construction for a new elementary school building near Kassem Village in Ash Sharqat. LTC Kyle M. McClelland, the Task Force 1-7 Commander, spoke to the students, parents and officials who attended and emphasized the importance of the youth and the role a quality education will play in Iraq's future. Sharqat's Mayor, the Honorable Muhsin Khalaf, echoed LTC McClelland's words and extended his appreciation to TF 1-7 for partnering with the community in this important endeavor.

Even as the soldiers of TF Lightning tried to establish a stable and secure environment in their area of operations, an Iraqi terrorist attacked the main gate of FOB Summerall on 1 June 2004 at 0900h in a dark blue BMW. The suicide bomber killed 11 civilians, including seven ICDC members, and wounded 30. Two 1st U.S. Infantry Division soldiers were wounded and evacuated to the 67th Combat Hospital at FOB Speicher, together with 18 Iraqis who were hurt. A gunner from an E Troop, 4th Cavalry up-armored M1114 HMMWV was moderately wounded as his patrol was entering FOB Summerall. He was protected from fragmentation by the gunner's shield, his helmet and the Interceptor Body Armor with SAPI plates. However, the tremendous force of the blast knocked the shield and the weapon from the mount into his chest, causing blunt trauma injuries. He was evacuated to the Landstuhl Regional Medical Center in Germany where he is recovering. The other Big Red One soldier received superficial wounds. Up to time of the transition of authority, five soldiers of Task Force Lightning were killed in action and at least 16 wounded. There were approximately 30 IED attacks, and nearly 30 non-detonated or incomplete IEDs were discovered. Today, IEDs are the major threat to the soldiers of TF Lightning during their daily missions around the city of Bayji.

Bravo Troop, 1st Squadron, 4th U.S. Cavalry does not habitually belong to Task Force 1-7 but was sent to FOB Summerall on a temporary basis by the Division Commander, Major General Batiste. The Bulldog troop is composed of two M3A2 ODS Bradley-equipped scout platoons, two M1A1 AIM Abrams tank platoons and an M1064A3 120mm mortar section.

In the light platoons of the ground scout troops, the M3A2 ODS Bradley CFVs operate in pairs. Here a pair is seen in the vicinity of Bayji during a reconnaissance mission. While the first vehicle is advancing to reach a new position, its buddy provides cover with the 25mm M242 Bushmaster gun. The Cavalry Fighting Vehicles of the 1st Squadron, 4th Cavalry Regiment (based in Schweinfurt, Germany) were also equipped with the new Explosive Reactive Armor after their arrival in Kuwait in February 2004.

Frontal view of an M3A2 ODS Bradley of Bravo Troop, 1st Squadron, 4th Cavalry Regiment. The vehicle has taken up a position on a hilltop outside of Bayji. From here the crew has maximum visibility and can use the 25mm main gun, as well as the TOW anti-tank guided-missile system, which has a maximum range of 3,750 meters (4,100 yards).

All the M3A2s of the "Quarterhorse" are brought up to the ODS standard and fitted with the Explosive Reactive Armor. The 608 hp Cummins VTA-903T turbo-diesel engine with 14.3-liter capacity provides the M3A2 ODS a maximum speed of 56km/h (35mph).

This Bradley commander monitors the vicinity of Bayji during a reconnaissance mission. Like the dismounts, CFV crews also wear the Interceptor Body Armor with Small Arms Insert Plate for protection against small arms fire and IEDs.

One of the most important jobs for Task Force 1-7, as well as all of the Multinational Force-Iraq area, is route clearance of Highway 1. This consists of deliberately clearing the highway of mines, IEDs and any anti-Coalition forces. TF 1-7 also executed and supervised traffic control points along Highway 1 that were primarily run by the Iraqi Civil Defense Corps and Iraqi National Police.

During Operation "Iraqi Freedom 2," a lot of Heavy Equipment Transporter System (HETS) are used to transport tanks and other heavy tracked and wheeled vehicles to minimize wear of the vehicles. The M1070 tractor and M1000 semi-trailer replaces the M911/M747 HET system as the Army's latest model HETS. The HETS was developed to accommodate the increased weight of the M1 Abrams family of main battle tanks. Unlike previous HETS, the M1070 is designed to carry both the tank and its crew.

Sometimes the combat patrols of Task Force 1-7 establish traffic control points on Highway 1 to search vehicles for illegal weapons, ammunition and IEDs. Here, while the gunner monitors the traffic, the dismounts search for suspicious vehicles, which they would pull out of line for a detailed search. Note the armor plates attached to the driver's door.

Like many of his soldiers, Sergeant First Class Travis also affixed the M68 reflex sight on his weapon with a cord. This procedure indicates that the soldiers do not really trust the Picatinny mount. Note the clipped ammunition magazines and the special load-bearing vest.

While one soldier conducts a detailed body check, the other provides security with his 5.56mm M16A4 rifle at the ready. To prevent the Iraqi civilians being searched at the traffic control point from seeing what areas of their vehicles the U.S. soldiers are inspecting, they are made to stand with the backs to their vehicles during the entire procedure.

Depending on the experience of the soldiers, they randomly stop trucks to check the passengers and their cargo for anything suspicious. This Iraqi truck is transporting plastic pipes from Mosul to Baghdad. Each soldier has been issued a CamelBak hydration system, which holds three liters of water.

This 5.56mm M249 SAW gunner secures his buddies while they conduct a body and vehicle check on Highway 1 north of Bayji. Even though there is a constant risk of being attacked with small arms, mines or IEDs, this M998 was not equipped with the Armor Survivability Kit (or even some steel plates) to protect the crew

Every box and each suspicious area of the vehicles is very carefully checked by the GIs. The Iraqis always have to open locked boxes or flaps because they could be connected to a booby trap. The most effective countermeasure against IEDs is a balanced combination of physical protection and tactical conduct of operation. This becomes extremely difficult during prolonged peacekeeping security and stabilization operations under asymmetric warfare conditions in which regular forces must quickly adapt their tactical drill procedures to unfamiliar combat situations. Troops operating in such a high-risk environment must be able to improvise their tactics to counter the evolving threats facing them.

This TF 1-7 soldier looks at a crater left by an IED that exploded along Highway 1. IEDs can be prepared almost anywhere, with materials that can be acquired from agricultural and medical supplies. Because they are not based on standard production formula, IEDs are more difficult to track and detect. When constructed properly, IEDs can defeat even highly protected threats, including main battle tanks and heavily armored bulldozers. Some IEDs utilize very heavy explosive devices that are buried below the surface of unpaved or paved roads, where they are covered, waiting to be activated by remote control. Such activation is usually dependent on opportunity.

The Long Range Advanced Scout Surveillance System is a long-range multi-sensor system designed for use by U.S. Army scouts. It provides real-time capability to detect, recognize, identify, and pinpoint distant target locations. The LRAS3 enables heavy battalion and regimental scouts like the ones of the 1st Squadron, 4th Cavalry Regiment to conduct 24-hour reconnaissance and surveillance missions while remaining outside threat acquisition and engagement ranges. The LRAS3's precise far target location capability is provided by an advanced second-generation forward-looking infrared (FLIR) sensor, a global positioning interferometer, an eye-safe laser range finder, and a television camera. The system can be mounted on the HMMWV, or used on a tripod for dismounted missions. Note the Elcan M145 sight attached to the 5.56mm M249 SAW.

This D7 bulldozer grades the shoulder of the K2 By-pass to prevent Iraqi insurgents from planting IEDs and mines. The D7 is a fully tracked, low speed, medium drawbar-pull bulldozer with a ripper or winch. The rebuild program, which brings the vehicles back to their original performance specifications, is expected to extend the service life by 15 years, and will yield cost savings over a new acquisition.

Today, the 1st Squadron, 4th U.S. Cavalry is equipped with the advanced M1A1 AIM Abrams main battle tank. The 1,500-hp Lycoming Textron AGT-1500 multi-fuel turbine engine provides the 63-ton tank with a maximum speed of 67 km/h (42mph) and a cruising range of nearly 466 km (289 miles), depending on terrain conditions. Unlike others, this engine has the advantage of being extremely quiet. Note the concertina wire attached to the sideskirt and the red and white cavalry guidon on the smoke grenade stowage box.

As tank commander of an M1A1 AIM, SSG Vermont sits on the right side of the turret and has overall responsibility for the operation of the tank. His cupola has eight vision blocks and a hatch that can be opened in three positions and which is capable of rotating 360° in power or manual mode. He is also provided with an optical extension for the gunner's primary sight, affording him the same view, and an override that allows him to take control of the turret and fire the weapons at any time. The M1A1 AIM still has no independent sight for the commander as does the German Leopard 2A5 MBT. The M1A1 AIM's crewmembers also wear the Interceptor Body Armor during missions in Iraq.

The main armament of the M1A1 AIM Abrams main battle tank is the well-known 120mm M256 smoothbore gun developed by Rheinmetall Landsysteme GmbH of Germany, which fires a variety of ammunition types. It is equipped with a thermal shroud, bore evacuator and a muzzle reference sensor to compensate for gun tube drop. The M1A1 AIM carries 40 rounds of 120mm ammunition, 34 in the turret bustle and six in a rear hull box. The commander has a .50-cal. Browning M2 machine gun on a powered rotary platform and equipped with a x3 magnification sight. This M1A1 AIM is fitted with Combat Identification Panels on the front and side of the turret to prevent friendly fire.

The suspension consists of seven road wheels, with the idler in front, drive sprocket in the rear and two return rollers. The number 1, 2 and 7 road wheels are provided with hydraulic rotary shocks and bump stops that allow 38cm (15 in) of travel, almost double that of the M60 MBT. This suspension gives the M1A1 AIM previously unheard of cross-country performance and a very soft ride, helping it to live up to the nickname some troops give it of the "Combat Cadillac." The T-158 track is rubber with steel pins and end connectors with replaceable pads. Note the stowage box attached to the turret stowage rack.

The hull and turret are protected by advanced armor similar to the Chobham armor developed by the UK Ministry of Defence. To provide a higher level of protection against anti-tank weapons, the M1A1 AIM tank also incorporates steel-encased depleted uranium armor. The tank is equipped with an automatic Halon fire extinguishing system that is activated within two milliseconds of an outbreak of fire and extinguishes it within 250 milliseconds. Armor bulkheads separate the crew compartment from the fuel tanks. On the turret roof there are blow-off panels that allow the explosion to vent upwards away from the crew in the event of an ammunition fire. There is also a set of blow-off panels under the hull for ammunition storage.

The AIM overhaul is the Army's under-funded program to sustain the nearly 7,000 Abrams tanks as part of the total recapitalization plan. AIM is funded at 135 tanks per year, which translates into a 12-year rebuild cycle for the active component. As the M1A2 fleet ages, the Army must expand AIM to include about 90 M1A2 SEPs per year beginning in 2012. With a 20-year rebuild cycle for the reserve component, the Army will also have to implement a 90-tanks-per-year program beginning in 2006. With the AIM program, the M1A1 tanks are completely remanufactured, resulting in nearly new tanks. Note the lights attached to the gun and the tow cable at the front of this M1A1 AIM, which was seen near Bayji.

Even as the soldiers of Task Force Lightning tried to establish a stable and secure environment in their area of operations, an Iraqi terrorist attacked the main gate of Forward Operating Base Summerall on 1 June 2004. He created a disaster by killing and wounding numerous people. (LTC McCelland)

This civilian contractor wearing a body armor and a Kevlar helmet tries to extinguish a burning Iraqi truck with firefighter equipment. There is nearly nothing remaining of a farmer's tractor and trailer in the front. (LTC McCelland)

After the attack with a vehicle-borne improvised explosive device (VBIED) on 1 June 2004, soldiers of Task Force 1-7 had to investigate the scene and secure the evidence. Vehicle-borne IEDs are explosive devices that use a vehicle as the package or container. These IEDs come in all shapes, colors, and sizes, which vary according to the type of vehicles available. Larger vehicles enable larger amounts of explosive to be used, resulting in a greater effect. The ways the devices function can vary as much as the package types but they can have the same common characteristics or indicators as other IEDs. (LTC McCelland)

The suicide bomber killed 11 civilians, including seven ICDC members, and wounded 30. Two 1st U.S. Infantry Division soldiers were wounded and evacuated to the 67th Combat Hospital at FOB Speicher, along with 18 Iraqis who were injured. (LTC McCelland)

3 June 2004, 0830h A patrol of four HMMWVs from 1st Platoon, A Company, 9th Engineer Battalion, which is part of TF Lightning, leaves Camp Summerall near Bayji through the main gate. Just two days earlier an Iraqi suicide bomber attacked the camp with a vehicle-borne improvised explosive device (VBIED), and the burned-out wrecks are still standing beside the main road leading to the gate, a reminder of this cruel terrorist act. Today's mission is the destruction of Air Defense Artillery (ADA) ammunition, which is buried in hundreds of caches all over a field just a few kilometers away near the K2 By-pass east of Bayji.

Unexploded Ordnance (UXO) and munitions caches have been a focal point for Coalition forces during Operations Iraqi Freedom 1 and 2. Anti-Iraqi forces have used the surplus of munitions stored by the former Iraqi Regime as a resource for improvised explosive devices and indirect fire on Coalition forces. OIF 1 began the cleanup of these ammunition supply points, but there was not enough time or resources to complete the mission. On their way to the ammunition site, the patrol passes some M1A1 AIMs belonging to the 1st Squadron, 4th Cavalry "Quarterhorse," which are providing security for two D7 engineer bulldozers grading the shoulder of the road to prevent insurgents from placing IEDs and mines. The Iraqis buried tons of ammunition in numerous trenches and foxholes all over the field near an oil refinery.

Like so often during the past weeks, the engineers from Schweinfurt, Germany, collect the ADA rounds and pile them in a big foxhole in the middle of the field for the further destruction. The soldiers, who were trained to operate large engineer equipment, quickly learned to identify the different types of UXO and how to safely dispose of them. They became skilled in area and point reconnaissance and familiar with the terrain and how the former Iraqi Regime stored its munitions. One of the soldiers wraps a long explosive cord around each shell in the foxhole. After nearly an hour, hundreds of rounds are ready for destruction by the 9th Engineers. To prevent anyone from getting injured, the U.S. soldiers block the road for a distance of two kilometers so no one can pass the site of the ammunition destruction. Immediately after setting a time fuse, the combat engineers leave the field in their HMMWV. A bright flash, followed seconds later by a loud explosion and shock wave, indicates the successful destruction of the ammunition. There is still a lot of work for the engineers as there are thousands of rounds of ammo buried all over the area beside the road. Destroying enemy weapons and ammunition is a very important mission because it decreases the amount of damage insurgents can inflict on Coalition forces with IEDs.

Because each round is stowed in a green plastic tube, it takes hours to cut the tubes and pile up the rounds for the destruction. Note the Big Red One combat patch on the right sleeve of this soldier, who belongs to Alpha Company of the 9th Engineer Battalion (based at Ledward Barracks in Schweinfurt, Germany).

These soldiers from the 1st Platoon, A Company, 9th Engineer Battalion "Gila Monster" destroy air defense artillery ammunition buried in hundreds of caches all over a field just a few kilometers from the K2 By-pass east of Bayji. Unexploded Ordnance (UXO) and munitions caches have been a focal point for Coalition forces during Operations Iraqi Freedom 1 and 2.

Like so often during the past weeks, the engineers from Schweinfurt, Germany, collect the ADA rounds and pile them in a big foxhole in the middle of a field for further destruction. One of the soldiers wraps a long explosive cord around each shell to make sure the ammunition is destroyed, effectively preventing the Iraqi insurgents from using it for IEDs.

The M249 gunner atop this M998 HMMWV fitted with custom-made armor plates and a special rack around the cargo compartment (which is produced by the company Johann Heim GmbH in Bamberg, Germany) provides security and monitors the K2 By-pass. While he performs this task, his comrades are preparing the ammunition for destruction. Note the rucksack attached to the front guard.

A bright flash that is followed seconds later by a loud explosion and a shock wave indicates that the destruction of the ammunition was successful. There is still a lot of work left for the engineers; thousands of rounds of ammunition are still buried all over the area beside the road.

3 June 2004, 1030h Today's mission for two M2A2 ODS Bradleys and two up-armored M1114 HMMWVs from 1st Platoon, A Company, 1st Battalion, 26th Infantry Regiment attached to Task Force 1-7 is a patrol in the vicinity of Bayji that includes the oil refinery, the frying-oil refinery and the power plant. They are searching for IEDs and showing their presence in the wake of the recent attacks against U.S. Coalition troops. After leaving FOB Summerall through the main gate, the combat patrol moves straight to the Bayji Police Station to pick up an Iraqi translator who would be supporting the U.S. soldiers during the following hours. The police commander and his assistant follow the convoy in one of the new police cars donated by the U.S. Coalition Provisional Authority (CPA).

The next stop is a traffic control point (TCP) established by Iraqi Civil Defense Corps (ICDC) members and Iraqi National Police (INP) police officers on Highway 1 north of the city. The patrol leader, Second Lieutenant Brooker (based in Schweinfurt, Germany), orders the M2A2 ODS Bradleys and the HMMWVs via his SINCGARS radio to take up defensive positions in front of the TCP. Their task is to provide security for the dismounted soldiers while they help the ICDC and INP check trucks and busses for illegal weapons and ammunition being transported to Kirkuk and Mosul. The machine gunners in the up-armored M1114 monitor the traffic for anything suspicious. Today's temperature of 45°C (113°F) does not make the job any easier. (The soldiers are very happy that their CamelBaks are filled.)

After 30 minutes have passed, the combat patrol has to leave the TCP because they still have to clear the road of IEDs from Bayji to the oil refinery. While the vehicles were driving in the direction of a bridge crossing Highway 1, the commander of the leading M2A2 ODS Bradley identifies a suspicious gray bag sitting beside the metal crash barrier. Losing no time, 2LT Brooker immediately orders the four armored vehicles to change direction and to drive directly over the four-lane Highway 1 instead of using the bridge.

The Bayji oil refinery (with its production capacity of 290,000 to 300,000 barrels per day) is a very important installation in the Task Force 1-7 AO, so the convoy stops in front of the main gate. The young patrol

This M2A2 ODS Bradley from the 1st Battalion, 26th Infantry Regiment monitors the traffic on Highways 1 north of Bayji and provides security for the dismounted Task Force 1-7 soldiers. They are helping the Iraqi Civil Defense Corps and Iraqi National Police check trucks and buses for illegal weapons and ammunition being transported to Kirkuk and Mosul at a traffic control point.

The combat patrol (which consists of two M2A2 ODS Bradleys and two up-armored M1114 HMMWVs) from 1st Platoon, A Company, 1st Battalion, 26th Infantry Regiment attached to Task Force 1-7. The patrol was tasked with patrolling in the vicinity of Bayji (including the oil refinery, the frying-oil refinery and the power plant) to search for IEDs and to show presence in the wake of recent attacks against U.S. Coalition troops. This M1114 was seen at a traffic control point.

Before the TF 1-7 combat patrol moved forward to the oil refinery in the vicinity of Bayji, Second Lieutenant Brooker got in touch with an Iraqi police officer at the Police Station in the middle of the city. Note the insignia of the new Iraqi National Police.

"Partnership." This young Iraqi National Police officer armed with a 7.62mm AK-47 rifle helps the Task Force 1-7 soldiers during their daily patrols in the city of Bayji located north of Tikrit. Note the attachment of the Elcan M145 sight, the flashlight and the AN/PEQ-2A aiming light on the M249 Squad Automatic Weapon.

Task Force Lightning arrived at FOB Lancer near Bayji on 6 March 2004. They were greeted with a warm welcome by TF 3-66 (Lancer), 1st BCT, 4th U.S. Infantry Division, from Fort Hood, Texas. After learning as much as they could from the soldiers of TF Lancer, TF Lightning took control of the area of operation (AO) in a battle-handover ceremony on 15 March 2004.

leader gets in touch with the members of the refinery security team. The INP translator supports him while asking about the situation around the installation and questioning if there have been any incidents during the last days. The situation during the first days of June was quiet, so the patrol leader decides to send his vehicles forward to the frying-oil refinery just three kilometers (2 miles) to the east. After a short drive, the combat patrol parks in front of the company's main gate, and the Second Lieutenant tells the guard at the gate that he would like to speak with the company manager. Without hesitation, he permits the Big Red One soldiers and INP officers to enter the facility; the manager is already waiting in front of the white administration building. After a warm welcome he invites the soldiers and the INP officers to follow him to his air-conditioned office for a small talk and some water and tea. (With the temperature rising to 48°C (118°F), the soldiers are happy to get some rest and enjoy a cool beverage.) The manager reports no incidents that the soldiers would have to handle, so the patrol leaves after only 20 minutes to check the last installation for today.

The Bayji thermal power plant, which is the largest in the country, is a major contributor to Baghdad's electricity supply. The road to the huge plant is very narrow and the commanders of the M2A2 ODS have to take care that their infantry fighting vehicles stay on the lane. It is as hot as a stove inside the Bradley, and the CamelBaks of the GIs are nearly empty now. Of course, the crews stored some more water bottles and coolers filled with ice and sodas inside their vehicles. It is summer in Iraq and temperatures above 50°C (122°F) are very common. Second Lieutenant

From time to time the Task Force 1-7 soldiers dismount to show force in the city of Bayji. The M2A2 ODS Bradley always stays close to provide firepower if necessary. Just two days before this photo was taken, an Iraqi insurgent blew himself up in a vehicle-borne improvised explosive device in front of the main gate of Forward Operating Base Summerall. The concertina wire alongside the road is used to protect a nearby police station.

Brooker is very happy when the security guards do not report any incidents around the power plant.

It is nearly 1345h and the soldiers of the combat patrol have had no lunch. They stop at a nearby KBR dining facility belonging to a pipeline construction camp to ask for meals. Here the soldiers of Task Force 1-7 receive a warm welcome by the KBR management and a delicious lunch in the air-conditioned dining facility before they have to head back to FOB Summerall in their unbearably hot vehicles. Shortly after the arrival in the FOB, the soldiers check their vehicles and weapons. For them it was just another combat patrol in Iraq. Today's mission clearly shows that the soldiers of Task Force Lightning not only show their presence on the streets around Bayji, they also try to get in touch with the local citizens and company managers to establish a stable and secure environment in their area of operation, as well as win the fight against anti-Coalition troops.

While 2LT Brooker was in a meeting with the company manager of a frying-oil company located east of Bayji and some police officers, this M2A2 ODS Bradley and a M998 HMMWV of the combat patrol parked in front of the main gate to provide security. Note the attachment of the tow cable on the front of the IFV and the space for a missing element of the Explosive Reactive Armor on the left sideskirt.

While some of the HMMWVs received the new Armor Survivability Kit, this M998 from the 1st Battalion, 7th Field Artillery was fitted with some steel plates to protect the soldiers against small arms fire. Unlike mines, which are triggered by pressure or magnetic influence, IEDs do not necessarily require physical contact or pressure for activation but can be activated by remote control, including wire, electronic signals or cellular phone. This mode of operation can be employed against selective targets, even on busy urban traffic lanes, as is repeatedly demonstrated in Iraq. In fact, the IED has become the symbol of the modern urban guerrilla.

Among the most dangerous threats faced by the Coalition troops are the IED ambushes and roadside bombs. In autumn 2003, responding to urgent calls from the field requesting armor suits for the soft vehicles, the U.S. Army launched a crash program to protect many of HMMWVs. The program proceeded in two parallel directions: 1) accelerated delivery of highly protected up-armored vehicle and 2) implementation of improvised near-term solutions that add some level of protection to the crews. Makeshift armoring of vehicles and ad-hoc, in-the-field solutions became temporary measures by the forces in theater.

A combat patrol normally takes between two and six hours, and each patrol consists of at least one of four armed vehicles (like this M998 with 7.62mm M240B machine gun). Even when the side of the HMMWV was armored with some steel plates, the windshield and the hood remained in the standard configuration. Note the taped reflectors on the side of the hood.

The infantry fighting vehicle in the foreground is an M2A2 Bradley, while the one in the background is an M2A2 ODS Bradley. The ODS increases system lethality over the A2 version by providing a Bradley Eye-Safe Laser Range Finder (BELRF). The addition of the Precision Lightweight GPS receiver, in conjunction with the Digital Compass System, enhances the ODS's ability to maneuver with the rest of the combined-arms team. The integration of GPS with the laser rangefinder also allows for a rapid, accurate call for fire.

16 March 2004

The Big Red One officially assumed command of Tikrit and the surrounding area from the 4th U.S. Infantry Division during a transfer-of-authority ceremony. During the day, troops of 1st ID and TF Danger conducted 15 patrols as the transfer of authority from Task Force Ironhorse began. Six of the patrols were joint operations conducted with the Iraqi National Police, ICDC and the Department of Border Enforcement. Weapons and equipment confiscated in raids and patrols throughout the area of operations of TF Ironhorse included 100 anti-personnel mines, seven rocket-launching tubes, 300 pounds of C-4 plastic explosive, 25 tubes of artillery propellant, 25 155mm artillery rounds, 100 sabot tank rounds, two anti-aircraft guns, 468 rounds of 12.7mm anti-aircraft ammunition, 84 boxes of other AA ammunition, and three improvised explosive devices.

Most of the HMMWVs used for combat patrols in Iraq are the up-armored M1114, which provide ballistic, artillery and mine-blast protection to the vehicle's occupants. The 5.5-ton vehicle is powered by a 6.5-liter, 8-cylinder, turbo-charged Detroit Diesel engine with 190hp. The principal modifications include an armor package, high capacity brakes, upgraded suspension and lift points, a reinforced frame, and a large capacity air-conditioning unit. The weapon mount, located on the roof of the vehicle, is adaptable to mount either the 7.62mm M204B machine gun, .50-cal. M2 machine gun, 5.56mm M249 squad automatic weapon, or the 40mm Mk19 Mod 3 automatic grenade launcher. The weapons platform can be traversed 360 degrees.

The up-armored M1114 was developed as a result of peacekeeping efforts throughout various parts of the world. A need was identified for an armored, mobile vehicle that provided a high level of ballistic protection against sniper fire and mine blasts. One of the great pieces of equipment that was used in Bosnia was this M1114 up-armored HMMWV. It is basically a standard HMMWV built on a heavy-duty HMMWV chassis with some extra ballistic protection. It is far superior to a normal HMMWV in terms of its ability to withstand a blast from a mine. Note the attachment of a spare wheel and the Light Vehicle Obscuration Smoke System (LVOSS) to this Task Force 1-77 M1114 that was seen near LSA Anaconda.

Soldiers from the 1st Squadron, 4th Cavalry and 1st Battalion, 26th Infantry Regiment discovered several weapons caches patrolling northwest of Samarra, in Tikrit and in the vicinity of Kirkuk. The Iraqi National Police reported that one individual was killed and four others were wounded when someone was attempting to make a bomb inside a house near Baqubah. The wounded were transported to a Baqubah hospital for treatment and questioned later by the police.

17 March 2004

A soldier from the 1st Battalion, 18th Infantry Regiment died and two were injured when their M2A2 ODS Bradley Fighting Vehicle overturned near Bayji at approximately 11:35 a.m. The injured soldiers were evacuated for treatment to the 67th Combat Support Hospital at FOB Speicher near Tikrit.

19 March 2004

A soldier from the 1st Battalion, 18th Infantry Regiment died the morning of the 19th as a result of injuries sustained when an M2A2 ODS Bradley Fighting Vehicle overturned near Bayji on 17th March. The soldier was one of two injured in the accident that killed another 1st ID soldier.

A soldier assigned to the 2nd Battalion, 2nd Infantry Regiment was electrocuted while laying telephone wires at FOB Comanche north of Baqubah. He was evacuated to the 31st Combat Support Hospital at LSA Anaconda, where he died from his injuries.

A soldier assigned to the 2nd Battalion, 11th Field Artillery Regiment died in Landstuhl, Germany, from injuries sustained on 11 March in a vehicle incident in Kirkuk.

20 March 2004

A soldier from the 1st Battalion, 26th Infantry Regiment was killed during a pre-patrol test firing in preparation for a mission near Samarra. During a raid near Kirkuk, TF Danger soldiers and Iraqi National Police captured two individuals suspected of planning an attack on Coalition forces. At about 01:08 a.m., soldiers from the 1st Battalion, 21st Infantry Regiment captured one individual suspected of planning an attack. Iraqi police captured the second individual, who was suspected of distributing posters with information about the attack, at about 01:37 p.m.

This sniper, who belongs to Task Force 1-77 from LSA Anaconda, is equipped with the old M21 sniper rifle, which was officially type classified M21 in 1975. The United States M-21 Sniper Rifle, which is a modified M-14 National Match rifle, has a high accuracy rating to approximately 822 meters (900 yards). It has a 20-round detachable magazine and is gas operated and air-cooled. Standard models include a 3x to 9x Automatic Ranging Telescope (ART) sight.

Even though the 1st U.S. Infantry Division mostly uses up-armored M1114 HMMWVs for combat patrols, there is still a need for the impressive and awesome M1A1 AIM Abrams main battle tank when it comes to intensive firefights with Iraqi insurgents armed with mortars and RPGs. The 1st Squadron, 4th U.S. Cavalry Regiment is used as the Division's Quick Reaction Force (QRF). Note the Combat Identification Panels and the lights attached to the turret of this M1A1 AIM that belongs to Bravo Troop, 1-4 CAV and was seen near FOB Summerall.

22 March 2004

A soldier of the Iraqi Civil Defense Corps was killed during a suicide car bomb attack at LSA Anaconda.

23 March 2004

An Iraqi child was killed and four soldiers and two Iraqi civilians were injured in two separate accidents. The Iraqi child was killed when she was struck by a vehicle in a 3rd Corps Support Command convoy east of Balad. The child died at the scene and her body was turned over to local authorities. Four 1st ID soldiers and two Iraqi civilians were injured in an accident involving two military vehicles near Tikrit the same morning. The soldiers were treated at the 67th Combat Support Hospital at FOB Speicher and were later listed in stable condition. The disposition of the Iraqis is unknown at this time. Two Iraqi police officers were killed and two wounded during an attack on a police station in Kirkuk.

24 March 2004

Task Force 1-77 soldiers captured seven individuals in a raid on two locations near Balad at 01:20 a.m. Anti-Coalition forces were identified at these locations earlier through unmanned aerial surveillance. Soldiers confiscated one pistol, two AK-47 assault rifles, one SKS rifle, and one artillery round. They also captured a rocket-propelled-grenade launch site. Soldiers from 1st Battalion, 18th Infantry Regiment located a weapons cache south of Bayji at approximately 10:00 a.m. Information from several Iraqi citizens helped the soldiers find the cache, which included 191 68mm air-to-surface helicopter missiles, 15 rockets and 35 fuses. The weapons were transported to a Coalition facility for destruction.

25 March 2004

A soldier from the 1st Battalion, 6th Field Artillery Regiment was killed and two others were wounded by an IED near Baqubah at approximately 08:20 a.m. The soldiers arrived at the scene after the ICDC reported the IED. As the soldiers investigated, it exploded. The wounded were evacuated to nearby Forward Operating Base Warhorse and were reported in stable condition.

Task Force Danger soldiers from the 1st Battalion, 14th Infantry Regiment detained two suspected arms traffickers in a raid near Tuz at 03:30 a.m. The soldiers detained the suspects after an Iraqi citizen identified them. The two are suspected of transporting large quantities of weapons between Nasiriyah, Baghdad, Kirkuk, and Hawija. Both were taken to a Coalition detention center for questioning.

27 March 2004

At approximately 09:50 a.m., Task Force soldiers from the 141st Engineer Battalion detained two individuals at a checkpoint and discovered nearly 20 million Dinar (approximately $60.000 US) in their

The UH-60L Black Hawk is the Army's front-line utility helicopter used for air assault, air cavalry and aero-medical evacuation units. Designed to carry 11 combat-loaded, air assault troops, it is capable of moving a 105-millimeter howitzer and 30 rounds of ammunition. The Black Hawk was first deployed in 1978, and its advanced technology makes it easy to maintain in the field. This UH-60L Black Hawk was used as a "battle taxi" for Brigadier General John W. Morgan III during his visit to FOB Summerall in June 2004.

car west of Samarra. The individuals and the money were transported to a Coalition detention facility near Samarra.

Iraqi insurgents killed a high ranking Iraqi police officer in front of his house in Kirkuk.

28 March 2004

A 13th COSCOM soldier was killed and another wounded as a result of an improvised explosive device attack near Al-Habbaniya at approximately 10:30 a.m. The injured soldier was evacuated by air to the 31st Combat Support Hospital, Baghdad.

Troops of the 1st Infantry Division and members of the Iraqi Civil Defense Corps conducted cordon-and-search operations in two districts of Samarra after an IED injured three soldiers.

30 March 2004

Task Force Danger soldiers from Task Force 1st Battalion, 120th Infantry Regiment discovered 30 mortar rounds and fuses and 15 rocket-propelled grenade launchers during a combat patrol east of Duywji at about 02:15 p.m.

This UH-60L Black Hawk pilot also relies on the advanced Interceptor Body Armor, even though it is not very comfortable to wear in the hot Iraqi environment. He also wears the Survival Armor Recovery Vest Insert and Packets (SARVIP), which is a Raschel knit and NOMEX fire resistant fabric vest with ten outer pockets and two inner pockets. The vest provides a means for attaching life preserver units, a protective mask blower, and it includes a rescue/lift strap.

The UH-60L Black Hawk has a composite titanium and fiberglass four-bladed main rotor that is powered by two General Electric T700-GE-700 1622 shp turboshaft engines, and has a speed of 163 mph (142 knots). The UH-60A Black Hawk is the primary division-level transport helicopter, providing dramatic improvements in troop capacity and cargo lift capability compared to the UH-1 Series "Huey" it replaces. The UH-60A, with its crew of three, can lift an entire fully equipped 11-man infantry squad in most weather conditions. Both the pilot and co-pilot are provided with armor-protective seats. Protective armor on the Black Hawk can withstand hits from 23mm shells.

31 March 2004

Five soldiers assigned to the 1st Engineer Battalion were killed when an IED hit their M113A3 armored personnel carrier in Habbaniyah. Soldiers from Task Force 1st Battalion, 26th Infantry Regiment discovered a cache north of Samarra at about 11:20 a.m. The cache consisted of 220 57mm rockets and one 155mm artillery round. An explosive ordnance disposal team destroyed the cache at about 01:30 a.m.

Soldiers from the 9th Engineer Battalion and 1st Battalion, 18th Infantry Regiment detained 147 looters near an ammunition storage facility south of Tikrit. Troops of the 9th Engineer Battalion observed the looting while they were escorting an explosive ordnance disposal team to destroy a weapons cache. Quick reaction forces from the 1st Battalion, 18th Infantry Regiment and the 9th Engineer Battalion were sent to assist and secure the storage facility. Nine individuals were transferred to a Coalition detention center.

1 April 2004

Three officers of the Iraq National Police were killed and two were wounded in Baqubah when they were attacked from a car during a traffic control operation.

4 April 2004

A vehicle-borne-IED attack killed one soldier assigned to the 1st Battalion, 21st Infantry Regiment and wounded six other soldiers in the vicinity of the police academy near Kirkuk at about 04:00 p.m.

5 April 2004

Iraqi National Police (with the help of Task Force Danger soldiers from the 1st Battalion, 120th Infantry Regiment) arrested two individuals in Mandeli at about 03:20 a.m. The police requested help from the soldiers after armed civilians were reported fighting in the marketplace. Iraqi insurgents killed a translator in Baqubah who worked for Coalition forces.

6 April 2004

A soldier assigned to the 1st Battalion, 77th Armor Regiment was killed and another one was wounded when mortar fire hit his guard post in Balad at about 08:35 p.m. The wounded soldier was medically evacuated to Landstuhl Regional Medical Center, Germany, and was reported to be in stable condition.

Soldiers from the 1st Battalion, 6th Field Artillery conducted a raid near Baqubah at about 04:45 a.m. to capture the leader and members of an insurgent cell. The soldiers

The UH-60L Black Hawk is usually armed with two 7.62mm M60D machine guns mounted in the windows behind the pilot and co-pilot on each side of the helicopter. The M60D is a lightweight, air-cooled, disintegrating metallic link belt-fed machine gun. This aircraft gun features spade grips, an aircraft ring-type sight and an improved ammunition feed system. A canvas ejection control bag attaches to the machine gun to catch ejected links and cartridge cases, preventing them from being ejected into the path of the rotor blades or turbine engine intake.

The tank company maintenance team from Charlie Company, 1-77 AR performs unit maintenance, repairs damaged vehicles and recovers disabled vehicles to the unit maintenance collection point (UMCP). Therefore, each of them is equipped with an M88A1, an M113A3, an M939 series truck, and an M105A2 cargo trailer.

Development of the Armor Survivability Kit started at the Research Development and Engineering Command's (RDECOM) Tank Automotive Research, Development and Engineering Center (TARDEC) and the Army Research Laboratory (ARL) back in October 2003. In only 20 days, designers and engineers designed, produced and tested the new door kit and the added protection panels. In this process, computer numerically controlled lasers, vertical mills and water cutting systems were used to produce the prototype sets. The prototype sets were mounted on HMMWVs and underwent a 2655-km (1650-mile) test drive, as well as extensive ballistic testing. On 13 November 2003, after redesigning the prototypes based on experience, the first 15 ASK sets were shipped to Iraq and Kuwait. By the end of November, 100 kits were already in use. Within two months after development began, the first vehicles in Iraq were equipped with the new add-on-armor package.

The M88A1 Medium Recovery Vehicle (MRV) is a fully tracked armored vehicle used to perform battlefield rescue and recovery missions. The M88A1 MRV performs hoisting, winching and towing operations in support of recovery operations and evacuation of heavy tanks and other tracked combat vehicles. It has a fuel/defuel capability and is fully equipped to provide maintenance and recovery support for the main battle tank family and similar vehicles. These functions can be performed in all types of terrain during all weather conditions.

detained 12 individuals (including the leader of the insurgents) who were suspected of conducting attacks against Coalition forces using IEDs, The individuals were transported to a Coalition detention facility.

7 April 2004

A soldier assigned to the 1st Squadron, 4th U.S. Cavalry died of a gunshot wound he received while on traffic-control duty in Samarra at about 09:25 p.m.

U.S. soldiers killed eight Iraqi demonstrators and wounded twelve during an anti-Coalition demonstration in Kirkuk.

8 April 2004

A soldier assigned to the 82nd Engineer Battalion was killed when individuals using an IED and small arms fire attacked his combat patrol in Khan Bani Saad at about 10:45 a.m. A quick reaction force responded, detaining two individuals.

9 April 2004

Three soldiers assigned to the 1st Battalion, 7th Field Artillery Regiment were killed and two were wounded when a rocket-propelled grenade struck their vehicle while on patrol on the south side of Bayji at 03:40 p.m. A soldier assigned to the 2nd Battalion, 2nd Infantry Regiment was killed when a rocket-propelled grenade struck his vehicle in Barez. Four individuals were captured in a raid near Hawija at about 10:16 p.m. The raid was conducted to capture or kill an individual suspected of planning vehicle-borne improvised-explosive-device attacks on Coalition forces. The four captured individuals were taken to Coalition detention facilities.

10 April 2004

A soldier assigned to F Troop, 4th Cavalry was killed and another wounded when 15 anti-Coalition insurgents attacked a reconnaissance patrol near Khalis at about 03:00 a.m. The wounded soldier was evacuated to a Coalition medical facility near Baqubah and was reported in stable condition.

Ninc Iraqis were killed and 14 wounded during fighting between Iraqi insurgents and U.S. Forces near Baqubah.

11 April 2004

A soldier assigned to the 2nd Battalion, 108th Infantry Regiment was killed and four others were wounded when a combat patrol was ambushed in Samarra at about 04:35 p.m. Soldiers from 1st Squadron, 4th Cavalry Regiment and AH-64 Apache helicopters were alerted to provide assistance. The wounded were evacuated to a nearby military medical facility.

Task Force Danger soldiers from the 1st Battalion, 21st Infantry Regiment discovered a weapons cache consisting of 18 60mm mortar rounds near Kirkuk at around 09:45 a.m. The soldiers found the cache after following up on information from some children playing near a Coalition base.

U.S. Forces and ICDC members killed one civilian and wounded six when they accidentally fired on a van in Baqubah.

12 April 2004

Task Force Danger soldiers from the 1st Battalion, 21st Infantry Regiment discovered 45 150-pound bombs near Kirkuk at about 12:23p.m.

13 April 2004

A soldier assigned to the 2nd Battalion, 2nd Infantry Regiment was killed and one civilian contractor was wounded when an IED exploded near their convoy south of Baghdad at about 12:30 a.m.

This M1070 Heavy Equipment Transporter System (HETS) belonging to the 299th Forward Support Battalion was seen in May 2004 at LSA Anaconda. The 8-cylinder Detroit Diesel engine 8V92TA DDEC III with 500hp provides the M1070 a maximum speed of 72km (45mph). The Allison CLT-754 automatic transmission has five forward and one reverse speeds. Since the convoys are attacked with small arms and IEDs nearly daily, the crews fitted their trucks with armor plates for the crew compartment. Note the overlap of the door armor over the crew compartment armor plates. The work of the 1st ID mechanics looks quite improvised and reflects the current threat in Iraq.

Task Force Danger soldiers from the 2nd Brigade, 25th Infantry Division killed one assailant during a small-arms-fire attack near Riyadh at around 07:30 a.m. The soldiers were conducting a route clearance mission at the time of the attack. Following the attack, they searched a nearby building and confiscated two AK-47 rifles.

Soldiers from the 1st Battalion, 18th Infantry Regiment confiscated a cache of weapons after stopping a vehicle at a TCP near Tikrit at about 01:42 p.m. A search of the vehicle yielded 11 60mm mortars, 16 fuses and 25 mortar charges.

14 April 2004
A soldier assigned to the 1st Battalion, 16th Infantry was killed and

The 260hp 6-cylinder Cummins 6CTA 8.3 Diesel engine with its 8.3-liter displacement, exhaust turbo-charger and inter-cooling (which is also used by the M939 truck series) provides the 13.4-ton M1117 Guardian ASV a maximum speed of 100km/h (62mph). In the middle of the vehicle is the electrically driven Cadillac Gage Upgunned Weapon Station (UGWS) with a Browning .50-cal. M48 Turret Mounted Machine Gun (TMMG) and a Rock Island Arsenal 40mm Mk19 Mod 3 grenade launcher, which has been used on the U.S. Marines AAVP7A1 for many years. This M1117 ASV seen at LSA Anaconda belongs to the 759th Military Police Battalion of the 89th Military Police Brigade, which is based at Ft. Carson, Colorado.

Even though the M109 trucks are ageing, they are still in use with the 299th Forward Support Battalion. The M109 belongs to the M44 series of 2.5-ton 6x6 trucks. This is one of the families of trucks commonly called "deuce-and-a-half" trucks due to the 2.5-ton off-road cargo capacity of the basic cargo configuration. They are also commonly called "multi-fuel" trucks because all but the earliest versions were made with multi-fuel diesel engines.

five wounded in two IED attacks near Samarra at around 12:00 a.m. The first IED killed one soldier and wounded two others. Nearby, a second convoy was attacked by another IED, wounding three soldiers. The wounded soldiers were transported to LSA Anaconda and were listed in stable condition. A soldier assigned to the 9th Engineer Battalion was killed when an improvised explosive device exploded near his convoy vehicle in Balad. 1st ID soldiers engaged and destroyed a truck west of Samarra at about 02:54 p.m. Task Force 1-26 discovered the truck containing 21 120mm rounds, 65 60mm rounds, two 40mm rounds, six RPG rockets, one sniper rifle, and one AK-47. Nearby, they also found a cache of three AK-47s, 25 30-round magazines, one 100-round drum, and one 40-round magazine. They destroyed most of the ammunition and transported the remainder to FOB Brassfield-Mora.

Task Force Danger soldiers located a weapons cache near Jalula at 09:05 a.m. Task Force 1-252 found 93 57mm rockets and 10 launch tubes. Soldiers secured the cache site until the cache was later destroyed. Task Force Danger soldiers conducted a reconnaissance patrol and located a weapons cache near Kirkuk. 1st Battalion, 27th Infantry Regiment found 262 33mm anti-aircraft rounds, 26 120mm mortar rounds, 23 mortar fuses, one 122mm artillery round, and 10 unidentified rockets. Recovered munitions were transported to a Coalition facility near Kirkuk for disposal.

16 April 2004
A soldier assigned to the 9th Engineer Battalion was killed and two were wounded when their military vehicle pulled off the road while on patrol in Tikrit and apparently hit a mine.

Two Iraqi citizens led Task Force Danger soldiers to enemy weapons in north central Iraq. In one instance, an Iraqi child led soldiers to an IED near Riyadh. The child told the soldiers that individuals from a nearby village had placed the IED. The soldiers found the device buried near a Coalition base. It was taken to the base for destruction. In another instance, an Iraqi citizen led soldiers to a rocket cache near Kirkuk, where soldiers discovered six 127mm rockets. Shortly after discovering the weapons, the soldiers were attacked by small arms fire, but no soldiers were wounded in the attack. The cache was secured for destruction.

17 April 2004
A soldier assigned to the 1st Battalion, 26th Infantry Regiment was killed when he was electrocuted while performing routine generator maintenance in Samarra.

18 April 2004
ICDC soldiers captured a suspected anti-Coalition leader near Tikrit at about 02:30 a.m. The individual, Hakeem Badour Khalaf, had been implicated in the deaths or injuries of at least three people, including two U.S. soldiers and an interpreter. He was detained and transported to a nearby Coalition base for questioning.

Some M978 HEMTT fuel trucks were also fitted with a special armor survivability kit to protect the crews from small arms fire and IEDs. Besides the additional steel plates, this vehicle also was equipped with armored seats for the driver and the passenger in the crew compartment. Note the armored front grill and the armored front light.

21 April 2004

Task Force Danger soldiers captured a suspected anti-Coalition insurgent and destroyed weapons sites during operations. Soldiers from the 2nd Battalion, 11th Field Artillery Regiment discovered and destroyed a rocket launch site near Kirkuk around 04:00 p.m. Two rockets were aimed at a nearby Coalition base.

In another incident, an Iraqi citizen led soldiers from the 65th Engineer Battalion and explosive ordnance disposal teams to a suspected minefield near Kirkuk around 07:00 p.m. The soldiers discovered two anti-personnel mines at the location. The site was marked for a later destruction.

Finally, soldiers from the 1st Battalion, 27th Infantry Regiment detained a suspected anti-Coalition militant during a raid near Huwijah about 10:30 p.m. The suspect was transported to a Coalition facility for questioning.

22 April 2004

Four 13th Corps Support Command (COSCOM) soldiers were injured as the result of an IED attack on their convoy near Al-Musayyib at approximately 12:25 p.m. The injured were evacuated to the 31st Combat Support Hospital.

23 April 2004

A soldier assigned to the 121st Signal Battalion was killed when his convoy vehicle hit an IED in Samarra.

24 April 2004

Two Iraqi National Police officers and two civilians were killed and 16 other civilians were wounded when an IED exploded outside of the 1st Infantry Division base in Tikrit at about 08:40 a.m. Civilian ambulances and fire trucks arrived at the site of the attack to transport the wounded to local hospitals. There were reports of small arms fire after the explosion. Soldiers from the 1st Battalion, 18th Infantry Regiment secured the site of the attack and began an investigation. No soldiers were injured in the blast.

Task Force Danger soldiers detained 19 anti-Coalition suspects and captured three weapons caches in north central Iraq. Soldiers detained 17 suspects near Tikrit around 11:54 a.m as they loaded fuses into a truck containing 30 mortar and artillery rounds. More than 2,400 additional rounds were found buried nearby. Soldiers detained another two suspects near Tikrit around 01:00 p.m., confiscating 60 mortar and artillery rounds. Finally, soldiers found and destroyed a cache of artillery rounds near Dibis around 03:19 p.m.

Iraqi insurgents killed four and wounded 16 people when they tried to kill a high-ranking Iraqi National Police officer in Tikrit with an IED. The Police colonel was not harmed.

Because of the constant danger when on patrol in Iraq, the U.S. military units have been forced to be inventive in fitting their vehicles with armor plates and machine guns. By the autumn of 2003, the U.S. troops had already lost several hundred soldiers in attacks; many of them were travelling in unprotected light vehicles. Most of the victims died from small arms fire, grenade attacks, IEDs, and RPG fire. This M998 is fitted with the latest Armor Survivability Kit and an armored weapon station with a 5.56mm M249 SAW, which can traverse a full 360 degrees.

25 April 2004

Eight 13th Corps Support Command soldiers were injured as the result of four separate attacks at various locations. Five soldiers were injured as the result of indirect fire at about 08:19 a.m. near Taji. One soldier was injured at about 07:20 a.m. when an IED struck a convoy near Dinaniayah. One was injured at about 08:55 a.m. when an IED struck a convoy near Samarra. Another soldier was injured at about 12:15 p.m. when an IED struck a convoy near Iskandariyah. The injured were evacuated to troop medical clinics and the 31st Combat Support Hospital.

28 April 2004

Soldiers from Task Force Danger detained six suspects and confiscated several large weapons caches during three raids in north central Iraq. In a 09:00 a.m. raid, soldiers from the 1st Battalion, 18th Infantry Regiment detained six suspects near Tikrit. The suspects were discovered loading munitions and scrap metal into a vehicle. The soldiers confiscated 30 120mm-mortar rounds and eight with fuses. The detainees were turned over to the Iraqi Police.

In a second raid around 10:20 a.m., soldiers from 1st Battalion, 150th Armor Regiment located a weapons cache near Mandeli containing 122 rocket-propelled grenade rounds. In a final raid at 05:30 p.m., soldiers

Because of the sand and dust in Iraq, the M1A1 AIM's 1,500-hp Lycoming Textron AGT-1500 multi-fuel turbine engines break down quite often and have to be repaired or replaced. But unlike others, this engine has the advantage of being extremely quiet. Even at full power, the turbine emits only a muted whine, giving the Abrams a tactical advantage over noisy diesel tanks. It runs primarily on diesel- or kerosene-based fuels such as DF-1, DF-2, JP-4, JP-5, JP-8, or kerosene.

The AN/TPQ-36(V)8, produced by Raytheon, is a lightweight, highly mobile radar set capable of detecting weapon projectiles launched at any angle within selected 90-degree azimuth sectors over 360-degree coverage. It can also be used to register and adjust friendly fire. Upon projectile detection, the weapon location is computed and is used to direct the counterfire from the M109A6 Paladin Howitzer firing batteries.

This M1097 belonging to the 5th Special Forces Group was seen in Forward Operating Base Paliwoda in June 2004. The vehicle is armed with a .50-cal. M2 machine gun and a 7.62mm M240B machine gun. Note the unique front guard and the stowage for the boxes of .50-caliber ammunition on the weapon station.

from 1st Battalion, 6th Field Artillery Regiment located a large weapons cache near Baqubah containing 1,500 14.5mm rounds.

29 April 2004

A soldier assigned to 1st Battalion, 63rd Armor Regiment was killed and one was wounded when an apparent IED exploded near their vehicle in Baqubah.

30 April 2004

A soldier assigned to the 367th Maintenance Company from the Missouri Army National Guard was killed when his convoy vehicle hit an improvised explosive device in Mosul.

1 May 2004

A soldier assigned to the 24th Quartermaster Company from Fort Lewis, Washington, died in Tikrit from injuries sustained on 30 April when his convoy vehicle hit an improvised explosive device.

2 May 2004

The commander of HHC, 1st Battalion, 16th Infantry Regiment was killed by an explosion while conducting combat operations in Anbar province. A soldier assigned to the 1st Battalion, 21st Infantry Regiment was killed and ten were wounded when their convoy encountered an improvised explosive device and small arms fire in Kirkuk.

At approximately 11:15 a.m., a patrol from Charlie Company, 2nd Battalion, 108th Infantry Regiment from the New York Army National Guard (assigned to the 1st Battalion, 26th Infantry Regiment of the 1st ID 2nd BCT Team) was operating near Balad when they were approached by a wounded man claiming to be an American. The man identified himself as Thomas Hamill, a driver for Kellogg, Brown and Root who had been taken hostage by anti-Coalition forces on 9 April. Hamill took the patrol to the house where he had been held captive. The unit conducted a hasty cordon-and-search operation in the area and detained two Iraqi citizens with one AK-47 rifle. The patrol called for a medevac helicopter, and Hamill was transported to a nearby military base, and then to Baghdad.

3 May 2004

Four soldiers assigned to F Troop, 4th Cavalry Regiment died in Balad when their military vehicle left the road and flipped over into a canal.

4 May 2004

Task Force Danger soldiers seized two weapons caches in northeastern Iraq. The first cache, which was seized by troops of the 1st Battalion, 18th Infantry Regiment near Tikrit around 01:20 a.m., consisted of 400 115mm tank rounds. The second cache was seized by soldiers of

2nd Battalion, 11th Field Artillery Regiment east of Raniyah around 07:45 p.m. It consisted of 92 100mm mortar rounds, 283 120mm artillery rounds, 50 12.7mm machine gun rounds, three 122mm high-explosive artillery rounds, and five three-meter rockets.

7 May 2004

An Iraqi provincial leader helped secure the release of two civilian contractors kidnapped by anti-Coalition forces near Ad Duluiyah around 03:30 p.m. The two were kidnapped while trying to recover a vehicle that had broken down earlier in the day. The provincial leader initially attempted to negotiate the captives' release but was unsuccessful. He then contacted the Iraqi police, who stopped the vehicles after a brief chase. The Iraqi police released three individuals after questioning them but detained one other. The contractors were not injured in the incident.

8 May 2004

A soldier assigned to C Company, 141st Engineer Combat Battalion from the North Dakota Army National Guard died in Landstuhl, Germany, from injuries sustained on 3 May when an IED detonated near the driver's side of his military vehicle. Also, a soldier assigned to B Company, 141st Engineer Combat Battalion from the North Dakota Army National Guard died in Balad from injuries sustained when an IED went off west of Samarra; another soldier was wounded. They were conducting an IED sweep when the attack occurred.

11 May 2004

Task Force Danger soldiers from the 1st Battalion, 113th Field Artillery Regiment detained an Iraqi Army soldier after finding sketches of a Coalition base in his possession during a shakedown inspection. The Iraqi soldier was taken to a Coalition detention facility for questioning.

A bomb was detonated at a market place in Kirkuk, killing three Iraqis and wounding another 25.

13 May 2004

Soldiers from the 1st Infantry Division captured two large weapons caches in northeastern Iraq. The first cache, discovered by soldiers from Task Force Tacoma near Balad, contained 37 rockets. The second cache, discovered by soldiers from 1st Battalion, 1st Aviation Regiment near Abayach, contained 300 rockets and two artillery rounds. Soldiers destroyed the second cache.

14 May 2004

A Kirkuk City Council member, Mustafa Kamal Yaycili, and another Iraqi civilian were killed, and four Task Force Danger soldiers and two civilians were injured in a vehicle accident near Tuz. The injured civilians were evacuated to a Kirkuk hospital. Their conditions were unknown. The

Each HMMWV of the 5th SFG in FOB Paliwoda received unique modifications. Note the prominent front grill, the different front guard and the armored doors. Of course, this HMMWV also has a weapon station on top of the crew compartment, but no weapon was mounted while this vehicle was parked at FOB Paliwoda.

Another photo of the 5th SFG HMMWV shows the mount for several fuel canisters and the 7.62mm M240B machine gun attached to the rear of the vehicle. The soldiers of the 5th Special Forces Group train the members of the Iraqi Civil Defense Corps at FOB Paliwoda.

injured soldiers were treated for minor injuries and returned to duty. Yaycili, a prominent Iraqi community leader, was a passenger in a civilian vehicle that crossed a highway median and struck a HMMWV driven by the soldiers.

16 May 2005

Soldiers of the 1st Infantry Division detained three suspected anti-Coalition insurgents and seized two weapons caches in Baqubah.

Soldiers from the 2nd Battalion, 63rd Armor Regiment detained three suspects following a mortar attack on a Coalition base.

Λ combat patrol followed a white pick-up truck to a house where the suspects were among a group unloading a cache of weapons. The cache included two machine guns, approximately 2,600 rounds of 7.62mm ammunition, 13 shotgun shells, one shotgun, and three AK-47 magazines.

Soldiers from the 105th Engineer Battalion discovered a cache of weapons near the city. The cache included 55 90mm mortar rounds, 40 82mm mortar rounds, 45 120mm mortar rounds, 20 107mm rockets, and one rocket-propelled grenade. The cache was destroyed at the site.

18 May 2004

A soldier assigned to B Battery, 1st Battalion, 33rd Field Artillery Regiment died in an electrocution accident in Bayji. A soldier assigned to B Company, 1st Battalion, 63rd Armor Regiment was killed by sniper fire while on a combat patrol in Muqdadiyah. An Iraqi citizen turned in 54 tank rounds to Task Force Danger soldiers at a Coalition base near Mandeli as part of a weapons buy-back program.

Troops of the 1st Infantry Division from the 336th Military Police detained nine suspects near the site of an IED explosion near Khalis that occurred around 07:25 p.m. The soldiers discovered two more IEDs and confiscated three AK-47 assault rifles, 100 rounds of 7.62mm ammunition, 12-gauge shotgun shells, one grenade primer, and several knives. No Coalition soldiers were injured in the attack.

19 May 2004

A soldier assigned to HHT, 1st Squadron, 4th Cavalry Regiment was killed and one was wounded when their combat patrol was attacked with an IED and small arms fire near Samarra. Another soldier was slightly injured trying to put out a fire caused by the explosion. The soldiers returned fire, wounding three suspected attackers. The wounded soldiers were evacuated to the 31st Combat Support Hospital in Balad for treatment and were reported in stable condition. Two of the wounded suspects were treated for their wounds and detained for questioning, while the third evaded capture.

An Iraqi citizen led Task Force Danger soldiers from 1st Battalion, 27th Infantry Regiment to an unexploded rocket near Hawija. The 80mm rocket had been fired at a Coalition base. An explosive ordnance disposal team destroyed the rocket.

20 May 2004

Both the 1st Infantry Division and Task Force Danger conducted 406 patrols and one raid. Fifty-seven of the patrols were joint operations conducted with the Iraqi Security Forces. Soldiers acquired one SA-7 surface-to-air missile and one SA-14 missile through a buy-back program. The raids and patrols produced 61 155mm artillery rounds, three 100mm artillery rounds, six rifle grenades, one rocket-propelled-grenade round, and six IEDs. The 61 155mm artillery rounds were found near Tikrit. Soldiers from the 141st Engineer Battalion destroyed the cache in place.

Elements of the 1st Infantry Division killed three enemy personnel during a series of attacks near Samarra. The soldiers were investigating a cache site when they were attacked at about 07:05 p.m. They regained contact with the enemy 20 minutes later and received RPG fire. Assailants attacked another patrol in the area with an IED. There were no U.S. injuries, nor damage to equipment.

Task Force Danger soldiers and Iraqi Security Forces conducted simultaneous overnight raids in and around Kirkuk. Thirty-six people were detained, including five suspected anti-Coalition-force cell leaders. Eighteen of the 36 detainees were screened and released within five hours. All operations were conducted without shots fired. The soldiers also seized

This M923A2 is also used as a gun truck armed with a 40mm Mk19 Mod 3 automatic grenade launcher. The armor plates were only fitted around the crew compartment but not on the dump body. Note the very well protected passenger side of the vehicle.

This M1075 PLS with a M1076 trailer was seen at LSA Anaconda, one of the main logistic bases north of Baghdad. The M1076 trailer is a three-axle, wagon-style trailer with a 16.5-ton payload capacity. It is equipped with a flatrack that is interchangeable between truck and trailer. The combination of truck and trailer provides the combined payload capacity of 33 tons. The flatracks are lifted on and off the truck and trailer by a hydraulic-powered arm mounted on the truck, which eliminates the need for additional material handling equipment. The controls for the arm are located inside the cab, allowing the operator to load or unload the truck in less than one minute without leaving the cab of the truck. The trailer can be loaded or unloaded in less than five minutes using the remote arm control. In contrast to the M1074 PLS, the M1075 is not equipped with a Material Handling Crane (MCH).

Photographed during a combat patrol in the city of Bayji, this soldier is armed with a 5.56mm M249 SAW with M145 sight and AN/PEQ-2A aiming light. All soldiers in Iraq wear the new Interceptor Body Armor (IBA) with Small Arms Protective Inserts instead of the old PASGT Body Armor issued in the 1980s. Note the elbow and knee protectors and the nametag attached to the IBA.

three RPG launchers, four AK-47s, and five grenades inside the Hussein Mosque.

22 May 2004

Task Force Danger soldiers confiscated several weapons caches found near Kirkuk and Jalula. A cache discovered at the Tal Ashtal airfield, south of Kirkuk, contained more than 50 artillery and mortar rounds and two rocket-propelled grenades. EOD teams destroyed the weapons. Several caches found near Jalula contained more than 80 rounds.

23 May 2004

A soldier assigned to the 1st Squadron, 4th Cavalry was killed and two were wounded when their armored HMMWV rolled over in Dawr. Soldiers from the 1st Battalion, 26th Infantry Regiment conducted a raid to capture a suspected sniper near Samarra. The soldiers raided two houses, detained one suspect and confiscated a cache of weapons and ammunition, including two pounds of homemade plastic explosive, 12 automatic rifles, two sniper rifles and a sniper scope, a shotgun, a handgun, a flare gun, and assorted ammunition.

24 May 2004

Soldiers discovered about 100 munitions and a minefield near Kirkuk. Later, they discovered another cache of mortar rounds, rockets, military communications equipment, and an anti-aircraft weapon. In addition, an Iraqi citizen turned in mortar rounds, fuses, and an anti-aircraft missile. He was rewarded with US$600.

Six anti-Coalition insurgents were killed in Tikrit when members of a 1st Infantry Division patrol returned fire after a series of attacks on them starting around 09:30 p.m. The attacks included small arms fire, rocket-propelled grenades, mortars, and IEDs. One soldier was slightly wounded and returned to duty. Iraqi insurgents conducted a bomb attack on an oil pipeline between Kirkuk and Dibris.

25 May 2004

Battalions from the 1st Infantry Division seized more than 1,000 munitions found in several caches near Tikrit on 25 and 26 May. In two

instances, Iraqi citizens provided information to Task Force Danger. In the first instance, an Iraqi's information led soldiers from the 1st Battalion, 252nd Armor Regiment to a cache near Jalula. The cache consisted of a rocket-propelled-grenade launcher with two grenades, a box of .50-caliber ammunition and three boxes of fuses. The soldiers also confiscated two AK-47s during their search on 25 May. Another citizen's help led soldiers of the 2nd Battalion, 63rd Armor Regiment to more than 358 rockets, which the Battalion destroyed on 26 May.

28 May 2004

Soldiers from the 1st Battalion, 26th Infantry Regiment destroyed a car bomb near Samarra. They found three 155mm rounds in the rear seat with batteries and a radio receiver hooked to the rounds.

Soldiers from the 1st Infantry Division returned fire and wounded an attacker who had fired a rocket-propelled grenade at them. The attacker was transported to a Coalition medical facility and will be detained for questioning.

ICDC soldiers turned in an IED to members of 1st Battalion, 27th Infantry Regiment that consisted of four 152mm artillery rounds and two 250-pound bombs.

30 May 2004

Soldiers from the 1st Battalion, 21st Infantry Regiment led explosive ordnance disposal teams to a weapons cache near Kirkuk. The EOD teams recovered more than 70 artillery and mortar rounds, 23 anti-tank munitions, an anti-personnel mine, and three hand grenades. While the EOD team was at the site, an Iraqi child brought one SA-7 surface-to-air missile to the soldiers.

1 June 2004

A soldier assigned to D Battery, 4th Battalion, 3rd Air Defense Artillery was killed when an Avenger air-defense vehicle rolled over in Anbar province. Men from the 1st Infantry Division detained two individuals and confiscated several weapons caches throughout north central Iraq. Soldiers discovered a total of six caches near Mansuriyah,

Some of the M1075 PLS are armed with machine guns and used as gun trucks. Note the improvised armor welded onto a flatrack. This PLS belonging to the 369th Transportation Company is also equipped with a Container Handling Unit (CHU).

This M1070 HET was used to transport one of the new up-armored M9 Dozer bulldozers. The U.S. Army has purchased several D9 armor kits from the Israeli Defense Force and used them to produce similarly fortified D9s. These are used to clear destroyed vehicles from roads, dig moats, erect earthen barriers, and construct field fortifications. D9s have also been used to raze houses that hosted snipers who shot at Coalition forces. The armored D9 Dozer provides armor protection to the mechanical systems and to the operator cabin. The operator is protected by bulletproof glass against bombs and machinegun- and sniper fire.

Baqubah, Tikrit, and Balad. The caches contained more than 400 artillery rounds, 101 anti-aircraft rounds, 57 mortar rounds, 47 rocket-propelled grenades, an RPG launcher, a machine gun, and other munitions.

2 June 2004

A mortar impacted and started a fire at a Coalition base near Kirkuk. There were no reports of injuries and the fire has since been controlled. The fire spread to an ammunition holding area, detonating the ammunition stored there. As a precaution, a nearby detention facility was evacuated. Damage to the ammunition holding area is being assessed

3 June 2004

Two Iraqis were detained following an indirect fire attack on a U.S. patrol near Abayach. The patrol detained the two people near the point where the attack originated. The pair was taken to a nearby Coalition base, where one tested positive for traces of explosives.

5 June 2004

One civilian contract driver died and one 13th Corps Support Command (COSCOM) soldier was injured as the result of an IED attack on their convoy near Haditha. The injured solider was evacuated by air to the 31st Combat Support Hospital and further evacuated to Landstuhl Regional Medical Center in Germany.

6 June 2004

Soldiers from the 1st Battalion, 6th Field Artillery Regiment detained two individuals while on patrol near Baqubah. The patrol stopped the individuals and confiscated a pistol, cellular phone and a weapons card that was not signed by Coalition forces. One 13th COSCOM soldier died and one suffered injury as a result of a mortar attack on LSA Anaconda. Both soldiers were initially evacuated to medical facilities, where one later died.

8 June 2004

A soldier assigned to HHC, 201st Forward Support Battalion was killed and ten soldiers and six Iraqi citizen were wounded when a vehicle packed with an IED drove into the gate of his compound while he was inspecting soldiers on guard duty in Baqubah.

Soldiers from the 1st Infantry Division detained eight individuals stealing munitions from an ammunition storage point near Ad Dwar. The soldiers confiscated 170 mortar rounds that had been loaded into three vehicles.

10 June 2004

Members of the 1st Infantry Division, local dignitaries and other guests were on hand for an Iraqi Civil Defense Corps Primary Leadership Development Course graduation ceremony. The class was the first to graduate from the newly opened North Central ICDC Regional Training Center at FOB Danger. After the graduation, the facility was dedicated with a ribbon-cutting ceremony. The new facility will also host basic training for ICDC soldiers. Task Force Danger soldiers found three

weapons caches near Khanaqin, Bayji and Tikrit.

15 June 2004

The commander of the 1st Infantry Division, Major General John R.S. Batiste, recently set a target date of 1 October for the Iraqi Civil Defense Corps to take over security responsibilities for the Salah Ad Din province. The Division's 2nd "Dagger" Brigade Combat Team is currently responsible for the province's security. Soldiers from the 2nd Battalion, 2nd Infantry Regiment captured four individuals suspected of attacking Coalition forces during a search of buildings near Baqubah. The capture followed an attack on a Coalition patrol.

16 June 2004

Twenty-three people were injured in a rocket attack on LSA Anaconda. Two injured soldiers died of their wounds. Fourteen of the injured were evacuated to the 31st Combat Support Hospital, and seven injured were treated at the troop medical clinic. Air and ground units here responded to the suspected source of the attack.

18 June 2004

A soldier assigned to the 1st Battalion, 6th Field Artillery was killed by small arms fire as his unit was engaging the enemy in Buhriz.

This M932 truck is also used to protect the supply convoys on their dangerous tours through Iraq. A maintenance shop at LSA Anaconda welded on the armor plates, but the .50-cal. M2 machine gun uses a standard gun mount. Note the Mercedes Benz sign attached to the front grill.

The NBC RECON platoon of the 12th Chemical Company "Hellfire" has a platoon headquarters and three NBC RECON squads, each of which is equipped with the world's best NBC Reconnaissance Vehicle, the M93A1 Fox NBCRS. The platoon's mission is to support efforts for contamination avoidance within the Division. The NBC reconnaissance platoon is employed to gain information about the enemy and the area of operation that has tactical significance.

To counter the daily threat of IEDs, which have already killed and injured a lot of Coalition soldiers in Iraq, the 1st U.S. Infantry Division is now supported by Charlie Company of the 489th Engineer Battalion (nickname "Trailblazer"). The company is equipped with the Interim Vehicle Mounted Mine Detector (IVMMD) System. It consists of the Meerkat Mine Detection Vehicle (MDV), the Husky Towing/Mine Detection Vehicle (T/MDV), the First Mine Detonation Trailer (F-MDT), the Second Mine Detonation Trailer (S-MDT), and the Third Mine Detonation Trailer (T-MDT). This Husky T/MDV is driving on the shoulder of Highway 1 near Balad.

Soldiers of the 1st Infantry Division engaged and killed two anti-Iraqi insurgents who attacked them with rocket-propelled grenades near Baqubah.

19 June 2004

Between 16 and 19 June, 1st Infantry Division soldiers came under continuous attack in Buhritz. Following a meeting with city officials, anti-Iraqi forces attacked the mayor's office with RPGs and small arms fire. During the fighting, Coalition forces captured Hussein Al Septi, a known anti-Iraqi-forces cell leader.

22 June 2004

Two Task Force Danger soldiers were killed and one was wounded when their convoy was attacked by small arms fire near Balad. The wounded soldier was transported to a Coalition medical facility near Balad and was reported in stable condition. One insurgent was killed and another wounded when a 1st Infantry Division patrol engaged them after an improvised explosive device attack on a Coalition convoy.

Many of the Big Red One soldiers serving in Iraq in support of Operation "Iraqi Freedom" are around 23 years of age. While on patrol, each infantry team has one 5.56mm M249 Squad Automatic Weapon gunner. Note the M145 sight and the AN/PEQ-2A aiming light attached to the SAW. The folding bipod is mounded under the gas chamber, and the gun has provisions for tripod or vehicle mountings. The mounted weapon in the background is a 7.62mm M240B machine gun.

The 17.2-ton Buffalo Mine Protected Clearance Vehicle (MPCV) is a blast resistant vehicle intended to protect soldiers from the effect of mines blasts during route clearance operations. The MPCV follows approximately 125 meters (137 yards) behind the Meerkat MDV. The MPCV has a five-soldier crew. The MPCV operator drives the MPCV and stays within the marked path created by the MDV. The Buffalo MPCV offers protection against 45lbs of explosive weight under the wheels and protection under the centerline of the chassis against up to 30lbs of explosive weight. Ballistic protection against up to 7.62mm NATO ammunition is assured. This armor is upgradeable to protect against Dragunov AP cartridges. The vehicle is powered by a standard Caterpillar C-12 diesel engine. All MPCVs used during Operation "Iraqi Freedom 2" are equipped with an air-conditioning system. Fourteen Buffalo are currently in service with the U.S. Army in Iraq and Afghanistan.

This M977 HEMTT of the 1st Battalion, 77th Armor Regiment, which was photographed in a scrap yard at LSA Anaconda, was hit by an improvised explosive device that exploded below the front axle on the passenger side, killing one soldier. Note the impact holes from shrapnel in the crew compartment. The fire caused by the IED destroyed the entire truck.

The M1114 HMMWV shown in this photo was destroyed by an RPG-7 rocket-propelled grenade that impacted below the front passenger doors. Note the shrapnel damage on the armored doors and car body. This M1114 can now only be used for spare parts to repair other damaged vehicles.

A fire caused by exploding batteries in the turret completely destroyed this M2A2 ODS Bradley infantry fighting vehicle from the 1st Battalion, 26th Infantry Regiment seen at LSA Anaconda. Even though the fire melted the turret into the hull, the Explosive Reactive Armor packages did not detonate from the heat. No crewmember was injured or killed in this accident.

Supported by ANG soldiers from the 2nd Battalion, 108th Infantry Regiment, two EOD Specialists belonging to the 748th Ordnance Company try to destroy this T-72M1 autoloader near FOB O'Ryan. Improvised explosive devices built from 125mm tank rounds are still very common in Iraq, even more than one year after the beginning of Operation "Iraqi Freedom."

24 June 2004

Two soldiers assigned to the 1st Battalion, 120th Infantry from the North Carolina Army National Guard were killed and seven wounded when their M2A2 ODS Bradley Fighting Vehicle came under attack from small arms fire and rocket-propelled grenades in Baqubah.

About 30 insurgents attacked a Baqubah police station with small arms and RPGs about 05:40 a.m. Coalition aircraft dropped three 500-pound bombs on insurgent strong points. The home of the Diyala province's chief of police was set on fire while he responded to attacks around Baqubah. The police chief and an Iraqi Police quick reaction force responded to the attack.

25 June 2004

Iraqi policemen detained three individuals suspected of attacking the Patriotic Union of Kurdistan headquarters near Tuz. Four individuals were spotted in the vehicle used in the attack; one evaded capture.

26 June 2004

An Iraqi citizen turned in 110 anti-personnel mines and two anti-tank mines to the 1st Infantry Division.

27 June 2004

Soldiers from the 1st Infantry Division and an explosive ordnance disposal team destroyed an improvised explosive device near Baqubah. The soldiers discovered an artillery round connected to a keyless car remote device.

Soldiers captured a suspected Fedayeen cell member and weapon smuggler near Jalula, The suspect, Yarob Saleh Hasson (also known as Yarob Geresha), was detained for questioning.

28 June 2004

Fifteen months after the United States led a coalition to oust Saddam Hussein from power, and two days before the 30 June deadline for control to be turned over to the interim Iraqi government, Iraq became a sovereign country again on Monday, 28 June 2004. U.S. Ambassador L. Paul Bremer, who had overseen the Coalition Provisional Authority (CPA) since the fall of Saddam Hussein, signed the legal papers in the presence of Prime Minister Iyad Allawi and presented them to the Chief Justice of Iraq, Midhat al-Mahmoud. About a half dozen Iraqi and coalition officials were also in attendance during this historic event in Baghdad.

This M978 HEMTT fuel truck belonging to the 1st Battalion, 77th Armor Regiment based at LSA Anaconda was completely destroyed when it rolled over during a mission in Iraq. Now the vehicle is only used for spare parts because it would be too expensive to repair all the damage caused by the accident.

As of late 2003, 40 to 60 percent of all attacks began with an IED that was often made from 125mm rounds like the ones seen in this photo. Some of the attacks included direct fire attacks immediately following the detonation of the device. However, more and more IEDs were subsequently used as a stand-alone means to engage a convoy. Some of the IEDs have been remotely detonated using relatively simple, readily available, low-technology devices such as garage door openers, car alarms, key fobs, door bells, toy car remotes, FRS and GMRS two-way radios, cellular telephones, and pagers, which enable radio frequency command detonation. This implies that observation of the target area probably requires line-of-sight observation points in many cases. However, the adoption of using radios, cell phones and other remote control devices has given the enemy the standoff ability to watch forces from a distance and not be compromised. Besides the Light Vehicle Obscuration Smoke System (LVOSS), this M1114 HMMWV from 2-108th INF is also equipped with Combat Identification Panels (CIP).

A member of the 748th Ordnance Company EOD teams prepares the T-72M1 autoloader with C4 explosives for the final detonation to prevent Iraqi insurgents from using the explosives for IEDs. Note the throat protector attached to the Interceptor Body Armor.

Besides the improved armor protection, one of the best features of the M1114 HMMWV is the air-conditioning system installed on the left side behind the crew compartment. You really learn to appreciate the A/C system during a 50°C (122°F) summer day in June in Iraq. The launchers of the LVOSS are mounted on all four sides of the roof. Note the gun shield and the skull-and-crossbones marking.

These two New York Army National Guard soldiers provide security during the destruction of unexploded ordnance in the vicinity of FOB O'Ryan. The soldiers in the front are armed with the paratrooper version of the M249 Squad Automatic Weapon. Note the shorter barrel and the telescopic stock. The gunner in the HMMWV weapon stations mans a 7.62mm M240B machine gun.

This HMMWV, which is equipped with a shelter, is used by the EOD team belonging to the 748th Ordnance Company based at LSA Anaconda. Each EOD team consists of two soldiers. Note the front guard attached to protect the fiberglass hood.

This gunner attached an M145 sight to his 7.62mm M240B machine gun. After extensive operational and technical tests, the U.S. Army has selected and type-classified the M240B 7.62mm medium machine gun produced by Fabrique Nationale as a replacement for the M60 Series machine gun. While possessing many of the same basic characteristics as the M60 Series medium machine guns, the M240 system has a durability that results in superior reliability and maintainability when compared to the M60. Note the Picatinny rail fitted to the handgrip.

Normally, Charlie Company, 1-18 INF has 14 M2A2 ODS Bradleys, but the organization was changed completely during Operation "Iraqi Freedom 2." Now the battalion operates more like a light infantry than a mechanized infantry company. The 12 HMMWVs of the 1st Rifle Platoon "Cold Steel" include M1114s, M1025s and some M998s fitted with custom-made steel plates to protect the crews from small arms fire and IEDs. In the near future, the TF 1-18 HMMWVs will also be fitted with the advanced Armor Survivability Kit (ASK).

One of the main tasks of Task Force 1-18 since their arrival in March 2004 is to conduct combat patrols in the city of Tikrit both day and night. From time to time the combat patrol stops and the soldiers quickly dismount from their vehicles to search the neighborhood for anything suspicious and for Iraqi insurgents. Note the M145 sight, the forward handgrip and the AN/PEQ-2A aiming light attached to this 5.56mm M249 Squad Automatic Weapon. It is common practice to cover all openings with tape to prevent malfunctions caused by the dust.

5 June 2004, 2300h   Under the cover of night, a combat patrol from the 1st Rifle Platoon, C Company, 1st Battalion, 18th Infantry Regiment "Vanguards" (with four armored HMMWVs) leaves FOB Danger in Tikrit. The wind makes this 20°C (68°F) night a little bit more endurable for the soldiers wearing heavy body armor and helmets. The camp, which is located on a palace complex of Saddam Hussein, includes the HHC of the 1st U.S. Infantry Division; the 4th Battalion, 3rd Air Defense Artillery; the 101st Military Intelligence Battalion; the 121st Signal Battalion; the 1st Military Police Company; and the HHC, Engineer Brigade. In an ironic twist of fate, what once was a vacation spot for the former dictator now could be a model for the Iraqis in the development of life in the post-Saddam era.

Forward Operating Base Danger is also the current home station for the Headquarters and Headquarters Company and C Company "Charlie Rock" of the 1st Battalion, 18th Infantry Regiment, which are normally based at Ledward Barracks in Schweinfurt, Germany. Task Force 1-18 consists of the 1st Battalion, 18th Infantry Regiment; A Company, 1st Battalion, 77th Armor Regiment; D Company, 2nd Battalion, 108th Infantry Regiment; elements of the 1st Battalion, 7th Field Artillery Regiment; the 9th Engineer Battalion; and the 299th Forward Support Battalion. During the Operation "Iraqi Freedom 2" deployment, "Charlie Rock" is responsible for providing security in the city of Tikrit, and so the nearly 100 soldiers control a city of almost 30,000 citizens. Tikrit, located on the Tigris River northwest of Baghdad, is Saddam Hussein's birthplace, and his clan and tribe are still predominant there. There are still many insurgents and regime loyalists in the vicinity. In the early days of the U.S. presence, the Big Red One soldiers were attacked a lot more often than today. Now people give them information and tell them things like the whereabouts of bombs and suspects. The hot spots in TF 1-18's area of operation are the main road and 40th and 60th Streets.

Normally, C Company, 1-18 INF has 14 M2A2 ODS Bradley Infantry Fighting Vehicles, but during OIF 2 the organization was changed completely and the Battalion operates more as a light infantry than a mechanized infantry company. Now the company consists of the Headquarters Platoon "Regulators" with four HMMWVs, the 1st Rifle Platoon "Cold Steel" with 12 HMMWVs, the 3rd Rifle Platoon "Ruff Riders" with four M2A2 ODS Bradleys and two HMMWVs, and the anti-armor platoon with four up-armored M1114 HMMWVs belonging to D Company, 2nd Battalion, 108th Infantry Regiment from the New York Army National Guard.

At the moment, raids or cordon-and-search operations are only conducted when there is a proven surveillance or when the soldiers are looking for a particular person. Every family in Tikrit is permitted to own an AK-47 rifle and one 30-round magazine for home

Sometimes Iraqi interpreters join the combat patrols to help the soldiers communicating with the local populace and officials. Most of the interpreters are not from Tikrit because they fear their families may get threatened or even attacked by insurgents. The 1st Rifle Platoon soldier's daily routine normally consists of eight hours of patrolling in Tikrit and eight hours for the maintenance of the vehicles and weapons.

Early on, soldiers of the Big Red One in Tikrit were attacked a lot more often than today. Now people give them information and tell them things like where bombs and suspects can be found. The hot spots in the TF 1-18 area of operations are the main road, 40th Street and 60th Street. Because of the constant threat of danger, the soldiers always have their weapons at the ready when patrolling in Tikrit. The ladder attached to the hood of the M998 HMMWV is used to enter buildings during cordon-and-search operations.

security, but the weapon has to be registered by the Iraqi National Police and the owner has to have a registration card available while armed with the weapon. To provide a secure and stable environment in the city of Tikrit, the "Charlie Rock" platoons conduct daily joint patrols with ICDC soldiers from A Company, 201st ICDC Battalion. Because of the constant attacks against Coalition forces, there is a very strict curfew in Tikrit from 2000h until 0600h. In the past, U.S. soldiers were mostly ambushed with small arms fire, RPGs and IEDs, and sometimes even with mortar rounds launched onto Camp Danger from various launch sites.

Despite the activities of Iraqi insurgents, Tikrit and many other cities belong to the Task Force Danger soldiers at night. Protected by the darkness of the night, the soldiers of the 1st Rifle Platoon from C Company, 1-18 INF patrol through the city showing force and taking advantage of their nearly 100% night fighting capability, which enables

them to see the Iraqi insurgents but to remain invisible to them. Without headlights off, the HMMWVs drive through the streets of Tikrit to make sure that the citizens can live in a secure and stable environment. Because of their AN/PVS-7B and AN/PVS-14 night vision goggles, the soldiers see the city in picture of various green colors. Very alert, the machine gunners on top of the HMMWVs monitor the back streets and roofs for anything suspicious. Anyone who does not respect the curfew is detained and depending on the circumstances handed over to the Iraqi National Police or told to go home right away.

It is 2345h now and the soldiers of the combat patrol carefully check all trashcans, metal boxes, plastic bags, and containers beside the streets since each could be a deadly IED or booby trap. From time to time, the laser points of the AN/PEQ-2A, which are only visible with the night vision goggles, wander through suspicious back streets and doorways. It makes no difference to the soldiers of TF 1-18 if it is day or night. In case of an attack, they can respond with an armament that consists of 5.56mm M4A1 carbines, 5.56mm M16A4 rifles and 5.56mm M249 Squad Automatic Weapons. Supporting the dismounted soldiers are 7.62mm M240B machine guns mounted on the HMMWVs, and some rifles are fitted with 40mm M203A1 grenade launchers.

Each rifle platoon has three identical rifle squads. These rifle squads are composed of two teams of four soldiers each along with the squad leader. When patrolling in Tikrit, the soldiers of TF 1-18 are always aware that Iraqi insurgents may attack them with small arms or IEDs. Improvised explosive devices usually combine the effects of the blast, fragmentation, and armor penetration through the use of shaped charge liners. Camouflaged explosives frequently serve as roadside bombs. These devices are remote controlled, triggered by infrared, pressure bars, trip wires, or remote control. They are sometimes used to delay or disrupt the movement of Coalition forces into a secured area.

This M998 HMMWV was fitted with a very improvised armor of steel plates and a mount for the 7.62mm M240B machine gun fitted on the cargo compartment. In the event of attack by the Iraqi insurgents, the TF 1-18 soldiers would like to have as much firepower as possible to suppress the attackers. Note the SINCGARS antennas and the safety belt attached to the rear of this much-weathered HMMWV.

With its night fighting capability, and because of the enormous firepower of the 20 soldiers, the combat patrol of 1-18 INF is able to protect itself against any kind of attack from the Iraqi insurgents. The 1st Rifle Platoon is composed of the platoon headquarters with the platoon leader, the radio telephone operator (RTO) with a PRC-119 SINCGARS radio, the medic, and the platoon sergeant. Their armament consists of two M4A1 carbines, two M16A4 rifles, three AN/PVS-14 NVGs, one AN/PVS-7B NVG, two AN/PEQ-2A aiming lights, two M68s, and one ACOG sight. Each rifle platoon has three identical rifle squads. These rifle squads are composed of two teams of four soldiers each and the squad leader equipped with an M16A4 rifle, AN/PVS-14 NVGs and an M68 sight. The rifle team has a team leader, an automatic rifleman, a grenadier, and a rifleman. In the 1st Platoon, the team leaders are the ones who have the M203A1 grenade launchers attached to their M16A4 rifles. The team's armament consists of four M16A4s, one M249 SAW, one M203A1 grenade launcher, one AN/PVS-14 and three AN/PVS-7B NVGs, and two AN/PEQ-2A aiming lights.

The rifle team's armament consists of four 5.56mm M16A4s, one 5.56mm M249 SAW, one 40mm M203A1 grenade launcher, one AN/PVS-14 and three AN/PVS-7B NVGs, and two AN/PEQ-2A aiming lights. Since the soldiers are not wearing the load-bearing vest (LBV), the ammunition pouches are directly attached to the Interceptor Body Armor. Note Motorola ICOM radio and the M68 reflex sight.

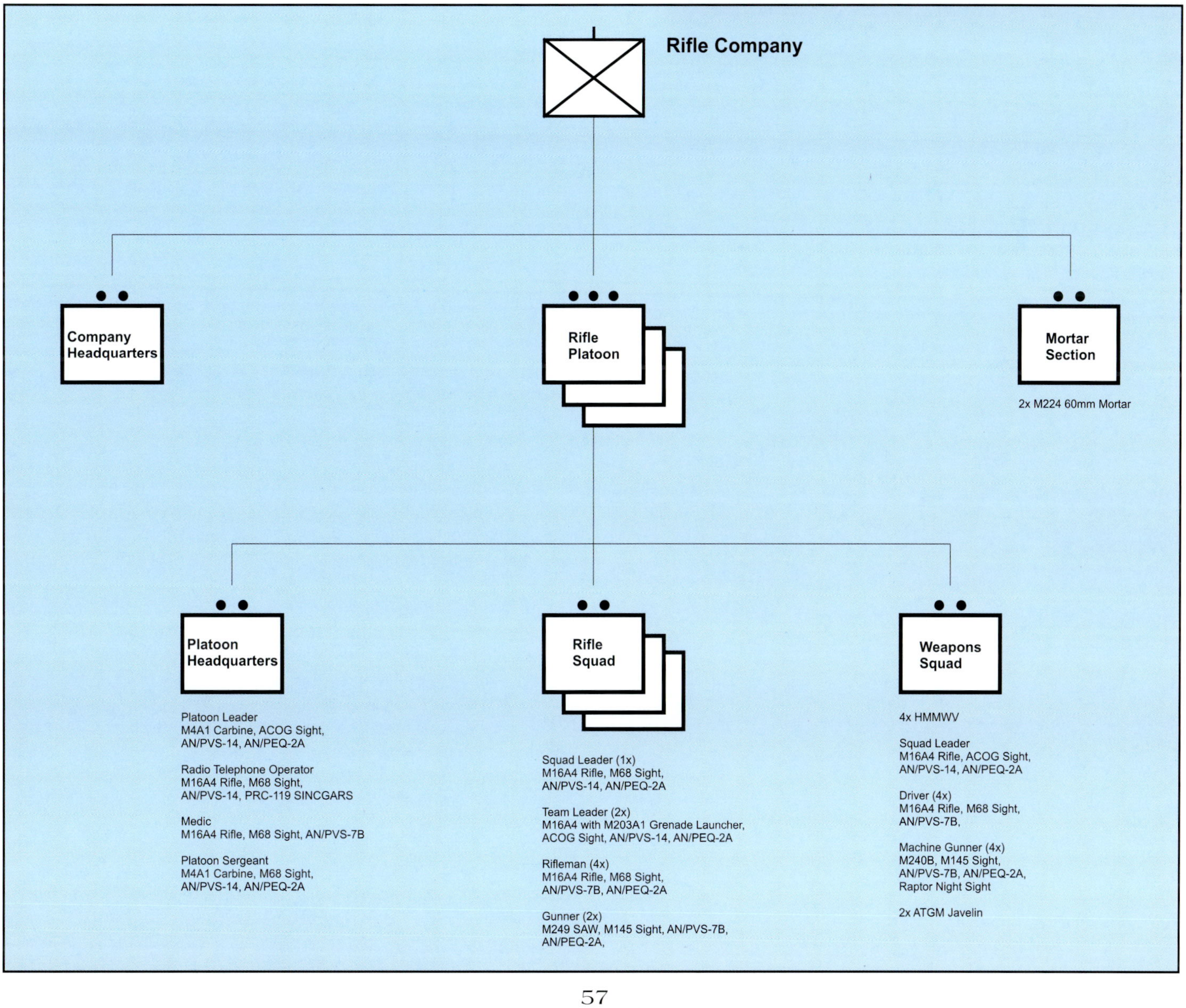

Rifle Company

Company Headquarters

Rifle Platoon

Mortar Section

2x M224 60mm Mortar

Platoon Headquarters

Platoon Leader
M4A1 Carbine, ACOG Sight,
AN/PVS-14, AN/PEQ-2A

Radio Telephone Operator
M16A4 Rifle, M68 Sight,
AN/PVS-14, PRC-119 SINCGARS

Medic
M16A4 Rifle, M68 Sight, AN/PVS-7B

Platoon Sergeant
M4A1 Carbine, M68 Sight,
AN/PVS-14, AN/PEQ-2A

Rifle Squad

Squad Leader (1x)
M16A4 Rifle, M68 Sight,
AN/PVS-14, AN/PEQ-2A

Team Leader (2x)
M16A4 with M203A1 Grenade Launcher,
ACOG Sight, AN/PVS-14, AN/PEQ-2A

Rifleman (4x)
M16A4 Rifle, M68 Sight,
AN/PVS-7B, AN/PEQ-2A

Gunner (2x)
M249 SAW, M145 Sight, AN/PVS-7B,
AN/PEQ-2A,

Weapons Squad

4x HMMWV

Squad Leader
M16A4 Rifle, ACOG Sight,
AN/PVS-14, AN/PEQ-2A

Driver (4x)
M16A4 Rifle, M68 Sight,
AN/PVS-7B,

Machine Gunner (4x)
M240B, M145 Sight,
AN/PVS-7B, AN/PEQ-2A,
Raptor Night Sight

2x ATGM Javelin

Interceptor is the model name for modular, multiple-threat body armor. Five sizes of the Interceptor, including front and back ergonomically designed plates, are being fielded. The Outer Tactical Vest (OTV) without plates weighs 3.8kg (8.4 lbs.) and protects against fragmentation and 9mm rounds. The Small Arms Protective Insert (SAPI) plates can withstand multiple small arms hits. The total system weight is 7.5kg (16.4 lbs.), which is 4.5kg (10 lbs.) less than the PASGT/ISAPO combination. There are attachable throat and groin protectors available for increased protection, as well as webbing attachment loops on the front of the vest, which accommodate the same pockets from the Modular Lightweight Load-Carrying Equipment (MOLLE). These features allow each individual soldier to tailor loads to meet the needs of his mission.

Besides an AN/PEQ-2A and an ammunition pouch, this soldier also attached a bipod, a forward handgrip and a scope to his 5.56mm M16A4 rifle. The AN/PEQ-2A target pointer/illuminator/aiming light (TPIAL) is a Class IIIb laser that emits a collimated beam of infrared light for precise aiming of the weapon, as well as a separate infrared illuminating beam with adjustable focus. It projects an infrared laser beam that cannot be seen with the eye but can be seen with night vision devices. It is also capable of projecting a much wider infrared illuminating beam from an integral illuminator. The TPIAL works with night vision goggles and mounts on various weapons with mounting brackets and adapters.

Protected by the darkness of the night, soldiers of the 1st Rifle Platoon of Charlie Company, 1-18 INF patrol through the city, showing force and taking advantage of the nearly 100% night fighting capability that enables them to see the Iraqi insurgents but stay invisible to them. This 5.56mm M249 SAW gunner uses AN/PVS-7B goggles attached to his Kevlar helmet. Furthermore, the M249B is fitted with a Raptor night vision sight, an AN/PEQ-2A aiming light and a forward handgrip. Note the camouflaged 5.56mm ammunition pouch and the three plastic ammunition boxes attached to the gun mount.

This mortar crew from TF 1-18 aims a 120mm M120 mortar in FOB Danger beside the palace used by Charlie Company, 1-18 INF. The M120 mortar is capable of providing close, continuous, accurate, and responsive indirect fire support to the task force commander in covering force and close combat areas of the battlefield. The M120 is also capable of providing target and battlefield illumination at night and during other periods of low visibility. Depending on the mission, it can also be used to fire smoke rounds. Note the soldier's blood type stencilled on the helmet band.

From time to time the combat patrol stops and the soldiers quickly dismount from their vehicles to search the neighborhood for anything suspicious or Iraqi insurgents. Luckily, the situation remains quiet tonight, just days before the handover of authority from the Coalition Provisional Authority back to the Iraqis. Last summer Tikrit was one of the worst towns in Iraq, a flash point of the emerging anti-American insurgency and a city that U.S. forces could barely enter in tanks without being shot at, much less walk through on foot. Today, it would not even make the Top 20 list of Iraq's most dangerous cities. As insurgents rose up in other Sunni Muslim-dominated towns (such as Fallujah, Baqubah and Ramadi), Tikrit has remained relatively quiet, drawing praise from U.S. officials and scorn from some Iraqis.

At the 1st Infantry Division's base camp there is an eerie feeling of calm these days. Mortar attacks, once a nightly occurrence, have all but stopped. Soldiers were recently told they could shed their flak jackets on base. The last combat patrol was hit with an improvised explosive device in May. American and Iraqi officials attributed the calm to a variety of factors, which included the U.S. military waving around dollars instead of guns, a weary population simply growing tired of fighting, and a shift in the Iraqi insurgency away from former Saddam loyalists (like those found in Tikrit) toward Islamic fundamentalists (such as those leading the resistance in Fallujah and Najaf).

Military officials say the December 2003 capture of Saddam also dealt a blow to the insurgency in Tikrit, which was showered with money and privileges under the former regime. Once the Tikritis realized they would never restore their old way of life, they began looking forward to what the Americans could provide. Up to the time of writing, the military

To provide security and stability in Tikrit, the soldiers of TF 1-18 also patrol at night. Tikrit, located on the Tigris River northwest of Baghdad, is Saddam Hussein's birthplace. Very alert, the machine gunner on top of the M998 HMMWV monitors the back streets and roofs for anything suspicious. The young GIs are equipped with the latest night vision equipment, which gives them a big advantage over the Iraqi insurgents. Note the fire extinguisher and the SINCGARS radio mounted on the back of this vehicle. The M998 is not even fitted with some armor plates, which is very risky for the crew when coming under small arms fire or getting attacked by IEDs.

The Raptor fitted to this M16A4 rifle is a 3rd generation night-vision weapon sight that utilizes the latest Ultra military image tube. Rugged yet lightweight construction makes the Raptor very reliable. It is the most accurate imaging device designed to withstand the rigors of combat use. Sighting is accomplished with a variable illuminated chevron ballistic reticle. The red-on-green reticle is fully adjustable for boresighting, and it has a separate control for optimal reticle brightness and contrast for all lighting conditions. Typical operating range is 2,216 meters (2,425 yards) in moonlight / 1,549 meters (1,695 yards) in starlight/ 768 meters (840 yards) in cloud cover.

had earmarked $58 million more for civic and community projects, including $43 million for the University of Tikrit. Since unemployment is one of the biggest problems in Tikrit, the Coalition forces try to give the citizens alternatives and jobs to get them out of the streets and help them to gain a better lifestyle.

All members of tonight's patrol have already been involved in fights with anti-Coalition forces in the months since they arrived in the city. Mostly, the Iraqi insurgents just shoot and scoot since they cannot match the U.S. firepower. Sometimes Iraqi interpreters join the combat patrols to help the soldiers communicate with the local peoples, the Iman or the mayor. For the most part, the interpreters hail from somewhere other than Tikrit or the vicinity since they fear their families may be threatened or even attacked by insurgents. The daily routine of the soldiers from the 1st Rifle Platoon normally consists of eight hours of patrolling in Tikrit and eight hours used for the maintenance of vehicles and weapons. The squad leaders use that time to train their soldiers.

After almost three hours on patrol, the soldiers head back to FOB Danger at around 0200h. Before entering the large camp beside the Tigris River, the combat patrol stops near an ICDC checkpoint and to see if there is anything they can do for their Iraqi comrades. More and more the Task Force Danger soldiers are handing the authority of the city back to Iraqi

Security Forces, which they have trained since the last three months. After arriving in the FOB, the GIs check their vehicles and weapons before they take a shower or simply relax in the huge palace made of sandstone and marble, which was once owned by Saddam Hussein. Tonight's mission was a typical one, and the soldiers of the 1st Rifle Platoon from C Company, 1-18 INF will not get much sleep; they will be on patrol in downtown Tikrit again early in the morning to provide security and stability for the city's residents.

On 1 July 2004, when Hussein appeared on television in a courtroom to face war crimes charges, emotions boiled over in Tikrit. An estimated 100 people demonstrated in the streets in favor of the former dictator. Iraqi police broke up the disturbance, firing warning shots into the air and making a handful of arrests. Just days later, on 18 June, two bombs exploded in Tikrit, killing a policeman and ending the three-month calm. Nowadays former Iraqi generals are working with the U.S. military and Iraqi National Guardsmen and go out with U.S. patrols. But some Hussein loyalists continue to hide and plot revenge. Iraqi and U.S. forces arrested a top Republican Guard general – a cousin of Hussein's – on 18 June who they said was helping to direct attacks on U.S. forces. Many residents watched this in sullen resentment of the Americans, their loyalty to Hussein undimmed.

Because of the constant attacks against Coalition forces, there is a very strict curfew in Tikrit from 2000h until 0600h. In the past, the U.S. soldiers were mostly ambushed with small arms fire, RPGs and IEDs, and sometimes even with mortar rounds launched onto Camp Danger from various launch sites. Anyone who does not respect the curfew is detained and depending on the circumstances handed over to the Iraqi National Police or told to go home right away.

Without lights off, the HMMWVs drive through the streets of Tikrit to make sure that the citizens can live in a secure and stable environment. Because of their AN/PVS-7B and AN/PVS-14 night vision goggles, the soldiers see the city in picture of various green colors.

The soldiers of the combat patrol from TF 1-18 are dismounted while checking out some Iraqi civilians who did not respect the curfew. The GIs have a nearly 100% night fighting capability, which gives them an enormous advantage over the Iraqi insurgents.

All members of tonight's patrol have already been involved in fights with anti-Coalition forces in the months since they arrived in the city. The Iraqi insurgents mostly just shoot and scoot since they cannot match the U.S. firepower. From time to time, the laser points of the AN/PEQ-2A, which are only visible with the night vision goggles, wander through suspicious back streets and doorways

Forward Operating Bases of Task Force Danger

During Operation "Iraqi Freedom 2," the units of the 1st U.S. Infantry Division and Task Force Danger are spread over the area of responsibility (AO), which consists of four provinces (Salah Ad Din, Kirkuk, Diyala and As Sulaymaniyah), to provide a stable and secure environment and enable the transition to designated Iraqi authorities and/or follow-on forces in preparation for Iraqi self-reliance. Camps like Logistic Supply Area (LSA) Anaconda are home to almost 17,000 soldiers, while small posts like FOB Paliwoda only have enough space for two reinforced companies. Most of the Forward Operating Bases (FOB) are isolated compounds built and used by Saddam Hussein's military and security forces. Some are located on the huge former Iraqi Air Force bases.

Accommodations vary in the FOBs. In most of the FOBs, the soldiers live in air-conditioned containers, while in others the GIs are still quartered in tents or old Iraqi buildings. On 13 June 2003, the Department of Defense signed a $200 million contract with the Kellogg, Brown & Root (KBR) subsidiary of Halliburton to build barracks for 100,000 troops in Iraq. The contract includes the set-up and operation of all housing and logistics to sustain task force personnel. The barracks is known as a "SEAhut," an abbreviation for "South East Asia huts" because they are so

similar to the quarters that were built for US troops in Vietnam. Halliburton has also constructed these facilities in Kosovo and Bosnia, and the designation has recently been changed to "SWAhut" to indicate South West Asia. This effort was undertaken through a task order under the long-term contract called the Logistics Civil Augmentation Program (LOGCAP). By June 2004, most troops stationed in Iraq had moved into trailer complexes. These trailers were obtained from local manufacturers, and there are hundreds of them arranged in rows. Most are single-wide trailers separated into two or three parts known by the slang term "hootches". Usually two soldiers are assigned to each air-conditioned "hootch".

The Moral Welfare and Recreation (MWR) facilities vary tremendously with the size of the camp. LSA Anaconda, one of the largest air bases in Iraq, has two swimming pools, a huge fitness gym, two movie theatres, and four cafeteria-style dining facilities (DFAC) run on the post by civilian contractors like KBR and ESS. The troops can choose from a variety of foods, including hot meals, fresh fruit, ice cream, cakes, and beverages for breakfast, lunch, dinner, and even midnight dinner. There is also a barber shop, and a Post Exchange run by AAFES (Air and Air Force Exchange Service) is also operated so soldiers can buy canned goods, snacks, electronic systems, CDs, DVDs, clothes, and jewellery. You may not believe it, but there is also a club tent in LSA Anaconda playing Techno, House, Old School, Hip Hop, R&B, and Country music in the evenings. KBR employees have their own DFAC, MWR facility and Internet cafe.

This huge and impressive palace made of sandstone and concrete belongs to Forward Operating Base Danger. It is currently the home of Charlie Company, 1st Battalion, 18th Infantry Regiment "Vanguards." While Saddam Hussein lived in unbelievable luxury, the people of Iraq lived in dire poverty. The statue in front shows Salah Al Din al Ayubi, a Kurdish warrior, who became the Sultan of Egypt and champion of Islam, and a legend in the East and West for his role in clearing the Crusaders from Jerusalem. Today, the stately compounds used by the U.S. Armed Forces are decaying because they do not take good care of the buildings and their inventory.

The Avenger Pedestal-Mounted Stinger system is a lightweight, mobile and transportable surface-to-air missile and gun weapon system. It is mounted on a HMMWV. The Avenger is designed to counter hostile cruise missiles, unmanned aerial vehicles, and low-flying, high-speed, fixed-wing aircraft and helicopters attacking or transiting friendly airspace. The firing unit consists of two turret-mounted Standard Vehicle-Mounted Launchers (SVMLs), a machine gun, a forward-looking infrared (FLIR) sight, a laser range finder (LRF), and an Identification Friend or Foe (IFF) system.

The main gate of Forward Operating Base Danger is secured by M2A2 Bradley Stinger Fighting Vehicles of the 4th Battalion, 3rd Air Defense Artillery Regiment "I Strike." They are fitted with Explosive Reactive Armor and protected by the Hesco barrier, a collapsible wire mesh container with a heavy-duty plastic liner. Just open it up, use a front-end loader to fill it with sand (dirt or gravel), and you have a protective barrier to protect personnel and equipment from enemy fire or bombs. Originally designed for use on beaches and marshes for erosion- and flood control, the "HESCO Bastion" (as it is officially known) quickly became a popular security device even before 11 September 2001. The device is named after the company that developed it over a decade ago: a British firm called HESCO.

In contrast, small posts like FOB Summerall near Bayji are still waiting for the KBR DFAC to open. They have been eating T-Rations since their arrival in March. Also, the MWR sites like the Post Exchange and the gym are much smaller and basic. But all camps have Internet cafes with computers and phones so soldiers can stay in touch with their loved ones. After signing in for a computer or phone, they are permitted to use it for 30 minutes before the next soldiers has the chance to use the equipment. Some units like HHC, 2nd BDE, 1st ID or 1-18 INF run their own Internet cafes, giving their soldiers the possibility to stay in touch with their family and friends more often and regularly.

Since the time the first U.S. soldiers established Forward Operating Bases in Iraq in April 2003, living conditions have improved from day to day. As of early 2004, U.S. occupation forces appeared to be deployed at approximately 50 locations in Iraq. An exact tally is impossible since not all operating locations have been publicly reported and some reported operating locations may have become inactive. The tally is also complicated by the multiple names applied to specific locations and the existence of multiple place names for contiguous locations. By late March 2004 it was apparent that the U.S. military was systematically renaming many of the existing Camps and Forward Operating Bases as Task Force Danger deployed to replace Task Force Ironhorse, which had served their time in Iraq. Camp Paliwoda, formerly known as FOB Eagle, was renamed in memory of Capt. Eric Paliwoda, who died on 2 January 2004 when an enemy mortar round scored a direct hit on his room. The following list shows the location of the Task Force Danger FOBs during Operation "Iraqi Freedom 2."

The soldiers of the 4th Battalion, 3rd Air Defense Artillery use their Avenger weapon systems to protect FOB Danger against attacks from Iraqi insurgents and to monitor the surrounding area with the advanced thermal sight. Each shift is eight hours and consists of doing a shift in the guard towers, slow reaction force (SRF) and the Quick Reaction Force (QRF). Soldiers pull an eight-hour shift in the towers around Camp Danger, and there are always two soldiers on duty in each tower at all times. They are the eyes that see everything that goes on outside the compound. The soldiers remain vigilant in the towers so they can report on any mortar rounds and rocket-propelled grenades that are fired at the compound. They also report Iraqis trying to infiltrate Camp Danger. Note the Armor Survivability Kit (ASK) attached to this Avenger and the tactical markings on the side.

Forward Operating Base Danger is located along the Tigris River 145 km (90 miles) north of Baghdad in the city of Tikrit. After the 4th U.S. Infantry Division departed, this base came under the control of the 1st U.S. Infantry Division, which was originally based in Würzburg, Germany. More than a decade after leading the charge into Iraq during Desert Storm, the 1st U.S. Infantry Division returned to the region to begin another chapter in its rich history.

The firing unit can launch a missile or fire the Browning .50-cal. M3P machine gun on the move or from a stationary position with the gunner in the turret. It can also be remotely operated from a location up to 50 meters (55 yards) away using the Remote Control Unit (RCU). The RCU consists of the same control units and displays that are fitted in the turret, including a FLIR monitor, Built-in Test Equipment (BITE) and hand control switches. The Avenger's sensor package includes a forward-looking infrared (FLIR), carbon dioxide, eye-safe laser range finder, and a video autotracker.

FOB Speicher is also home to the 1st Battalion, 1st Aviation Regiment "Gun Fighters," who are equipped with AH-64A Apache attack helicopters. This battalion Tactical Operations Center (TOC) is located beside the airfield in the middle of the FOB. On 24 February 1991, the Battalion helped the 1st U.S. Infantry Division spearhead the VII Corps attack into Iraq. In March 2004, the 1st Battalion, 1st Aviation Regiment returned once again to Iraq to support Operation "Iraqi Freedom 2." The sign in front of the tent symbolizes the tight bonds of the Battalion to their German home base.

1st Infantry Division and 2nd Brigade Combat Team

FOB Danger – Tikrit
HHC, 1st ID
HHC, Engineer Brigade
1st Military Police Company
1st Battalion, 18th Infantry
4th Battalion, 3rd Air Defense Artillery
121st Signal Battalion
101st Military Intelligence Battalion
106th Finance Battalion
415th Civil Affairs Battalion

FOB Dagger – Tikrit
HHC, 2nd Brigade Combat Team, 1st ID

This tower is the headquarters of Task Force 1-7, which is under the command of Lieutenant Colonel Kyle McClelland at Forward Operating Base Summerall, located near Bayji. It was named in memory of SPC Tracy Laramore and SPC Clint Matthews, who were killed in action on 14 March 2004 while serving with Task Force 1-7. By late 2003, a number of contractors had started moving in the FOB, including the Washington Group, Bechtel and Kellogg Brown & Root (KBR). They are each performing various missions: restoring oil, water, electricity, phones, and destroying unexploded ordnance.

FOB Speicher - Tikrit
HHC, 4th Brigade, 1st ID
1st Battalion, 1st Aviation
2nd Battalion, 1st Aviation
601st Aviation Support Battalion
264th Corps Engineer Group
216th Engineer Battalion
141st Engineer Battalion
12th Chemical Company
167th Corps Support Group
44th Corps Support Battalion
232nd Corps Support Battalion
835th Corps Support Battalion
701st Main Support Battalion
38th Personal Support Battalion

FOB Remagen – Tikrit
9th Engineer Battalion

LSA Anaconda - Balad
1st Battalion, 77th Armor
299th Forward Support Battalion

FOB O'Ryan - Balad
2nd Battalion, 108th Infantry

FOB Paliwoda - Balad
1st Battalion, 77th Armor

FOB Summerall - Bayji
HHB, Division Artillery
1st Battalion, 7th Field Artillery
1st Battalion, 33rd Field Artillery (MLRS/TA)

FOB Tinderbox – Bayji
E Troop, 4th Cavalry
1st Battalion, 77th Armor

FOB McKenzie – Samarra
1st Squadron, 4th Cavalry

FOB Brassfield-Mora – Samarra
1st Battalion, 26th Infantry

3rd Brigade Combat Team
FOB Gabe – Baqubah
82nd Engineer Battalion
1st Battalion, 6th Field Artillery

FOB Warhorse - Baqubah
HHC, 3rd Brigade Combat Team, 1st ID
F Troop, 4th Cavalry
201st Forward Support Battalion

FOB Normandy - Baqubah
2nd Battalion, 2nd Infantry

FOB Scunion - Baqubah
2nd Battalion, 63rd Armor

30th Brigade Combat Team
FOB Bernstein – Tuz Khurmatu
1st Battalion, 120th Infantry

FOB Cobra – Jalawla
1st Battalion, 252nd Armor

FOB Rough Rider – Mandali
1st Battalion, 150th Armor
105th Engineer Battalion

FOB Caldwell - Kirkhush
HHC 30th Brigade Combat Team
230th Forward Support Battalion
1st Battalion, 113th Field Artillery

2nd Brigade, 25th Infantry Division
FOB Warrior - Kirkuk
1st Battalion, 21st Infantry
1st Battalion, 14th Infantry
225th Forward Support Battalion

FOB Altun Kupri
2nd Battalion, 11th Field Artillery

FOB Gaines Mills
1st Battalion, 27th Infantry

This M994A1 maintenance truck was seen at FOB Speicher in June 2004. Among many other tools, there is a lathe installed in the cargo compartment behind the cab. The soldiers call the M944A1 the "Batmobile" because you can fold the sides of the rear compartment to the top.

The AH-64A Apache is the Army's primary attack helicopter. It is a quick-reacting, airborne weapon system that can fight close and deep to destroy, disrupt or delay enemy forces. The Apache is designed to fight and survive during the day, night, and in adverse weather throughout the world. The principal mission of the Apache is the destruction of high-value targets with the HELLFIRE missile. It is also capable of employing a 30mm M230 chain gun, and 2.75" Hydra 70 rockets that are lethal against a wide variety of targets.

The AH-64A Apache is a twin-engine, four-bladed, multi-mission attack helicopter designed as a highly stable aerial weapons-delivery platform. With a tandem-seated crew consisting of the pilot (located in the rear cockpit position) and the co-pilot gunner (CPG) (located in the front position), the Apache is self-deployable, highly survivable and able to deliver a lethal array of battlefield armaments. The AH-64A Apache features a Target Acquisition Designation Sight (TADS) and a Pilot Night Vision Sensor (PNVS), which enables the crew to navigate and conduct precision attacks during the day, at night and in adverse weather conditions.

For the most part, the soldiers of the Big Red One live in air-conditioned containers that are brought into Iraq by the contractor-company KBR. To protect the living quarters from small arms fire and artillery shrapnel, portable concrete walls and sandbags are put around and on top of the dwelling. Two soldiers are usually assigned to each container.

Located 80 kilometers (50 miles) north of Baghdad, FOB Paliwoda has the appearance of Fort Apache. An earthen berm traces the 2.4-km (1.5-mile) perimeter. Outside runs a woven wire fence topped by barbed wire. Beyond that, a ring of concertina wire encircles the entire base. The base is home to more than 300 members of the 1st Battalion, 77th Armor Regiment, which is part of the 1st U.S. Infantry Division's 2nd Brigade Combat Team. From the base, the soldiers bring peace and democracy to their portion of Iraq's Sunni Triangle, an area where support of Saddam Hussein is common. The base is near Balad, a town of Shi'ite Muslims who mostly embrace the U.S. presence.

This young specialist conducts gate guard duty at Forward Operating Base Paliwoda. The weapon in the foreground is a standard 5.56mm M16A2 rifle, while the one in the background is a 5.56mm M16A4 rifle. The main difference between the A2 version and the A4 version is the removable carrying handle/sight and the Picatinny rail integrated system used to attach flashlights, aiming lights or sights.

One Year Can Be a Long Time

As it looks right now, the soldiers of the 1st U.S. Infantry Division and Task Force Danger will remain in Iraq at least until April 2005 at which time they should be replaced by the New York Army National Guard's 42nd U.S. Infantry Division "Rainbow." Many of the soldiers are eager to return to their home stations in Germany. If you speak to Big Red One soldiers in Iraq, most will express a longing for their German wife or girlfriend, and for the delicious German beer and food. This is a very reasonable desire since U.S. troops are strictly banned from consuming any alcohol while they serve in Southwest Asia in support of Operation "Iraqi Freedom 2."

Because of the extensive withdrawal of U.S. troops from Europe, which was announced by President George W. Bush in August 2004, it remains uncertain whether the 1st U.S. Infantry Division will return to Germany after finishing Operation "Iraqi Freedom 2" or if the famous Big Red One will return to the United States. The soldiers of the BRO can only hope that they will not face the same situation as the 1st U.S. Armored Division, which was scheduled to return to its home bases in Germany in April 2004 but received a 90-day extension to help combat the surge in anti-occupation violence. This tour extension came at a particularly delicate time when at least 73 troops were killed in April, up to that time the deadliest month since the troops set foot in Iraq in March 2003. The advantage of keeping soldiers of the 1st U.S. Armored Division in Iraq for an extra three months – rather than bringing in an equivalent number from elsewhere – was that these soldiers had unmatched combat experience in Iraq. Today, the Army is so stretched by its commitments in Iraq, Afghanistan, the Balkans, and elsewhere that it has few, if any, forces immediately available to substitute for units in Iraq. But no matter how long the soldiers of the Big Red One have to stay to help create a stable and secure Iraq, they will always be stalwartly true to their motto:

"No Mission too Difficult – No Sacrifice too Great – Duty First"

Dedication

This book is dedicated to my friends serving in Iraq during Operation "Iraqi Freedom II":

SPC Loraine Soto (HHC EN BDE 1st ID); SGT Chris Dockery (HHC EN BDE 1st ID); SGT Patrick Johns (1-33 FA); SGT Ruel Thompson (1-77 AR); SSG Sebastian Rojas (1-77 AR); SSG Mark Vernon (1-4 CAV); TSGT James D. Leis (332 EAMS); SFC Rodney Nilles (1-18 INF); SFC Randy McGill (HHC EN BDE 1st ID); SGM Eugene Turpin (HHC EN BDE 1st ID); CSM Robert Winzenried (HHC EN BDE 1st ID); CW4 Richard Martin (HHC EN BDE 1st ID); 1LT Anthony Courtney (1-18 INF); 1LT Shawn Tabakin (2-108 INF); CPT William Coppernoll (1st ID PAO); CPT Robert Gagnon (1-77 AR); MAJ Steven Nettleton (HHC 1st ID); MAJ Debra Stewart (1st ID PAO); LTC Kenneth Boehme (1-33 FA); LTC Kyle M. McClelland (1-7 FA); LTC Courtney W. Paul (HHC EN BDE 1st ID); and especially my very close friend, SPC Kimmer L. Horsen (HHC EN BDE 1st ID), and my grandmother, Erna Zwilling (18.09.1911 – 15.08.2004). God bless you all!

Acknowledgements

I would like to thank the following soldiers and friends who provided outstanding support to help me realize this book:

SSG Sebastian Rojas (1-77 AR); SSG Mark Vernon (1-4 CAV); TSGT James D. Leis (332 EAMS); SFC Rodney Nilles (1-18 INF); SFC Philip Eville (1-77 AR); SFC Randy McGill (HHC EN BDE 1st ID); CSM Robert Winzenried (HHC EN BDE 1st ID); 1LT Anthony Courtney (1-18 INF); 1LT Shawn Tabankin (2-108 INF); CPT Randall Baucom (CFLCC/3A-FWD-PAO); CPT William Coppernoll (1st ID PAO); CPT Gagnon (1-77 AR); CPT Michael Kennedy (1-77 AR); CPT Ryan Rooney (1-7 FA); CPT Brian Lucas (CJTF-7 PAO); MAJ Steve Nettleton (HHC 1st ID); MAJ Debra Stewart (1st ID PAO); MAJ Richard Spiegel (13th COSCOM PAO); LTC Kenneth Boehme (1-33 FA); LTC James W. Dirkse; LTC Kyle MM. McClelland (1-7 FA); LTC Brian McNerney (USAREUR PAO); LTC Courtney W. Paul (HHC EN BDE 1st ID); Mr. Wolfgang Hertrich (DIVARTY 1st ID); and Mrs. Millie Water (IMA-E PAO).